W9-CQZ-898

Talking
About Text

*Guiding Students to
Increase Comprehension
Through Purposeful Talk*

Author
Maria Nichols
Foreword by Peter Johnston, Ph.D.

SHELL EDUCATION

Talking About Text: Guiding Students to Increase Comprehension Through Purposeful Talk

Editor
Jodene Lynn Smith, M.A.

Assistant Editor
Leslie Huber, M.A.

Editorial Director
Lori Kamola, M.S.Ed.

Editor-in-Chief
Sharon Coan, M.S.Ed.

Editorial Manager
Gisela Lee

Consultant
Joan Irwin, M.A.

Creative Director
Lee Aucoin

Cover Design
Lee Aucoin

Print Production Manager
Don Tran

Interior Layout Designer
Robin Erickson

Print Production
Juan Chavolla

Publisher
Corinne Burton, M.A.Ed.

The names in this book have been changed to protect the identities of teachers and students.

Shell Education

5301 Oceanus Drive

Huntington Beach, CA 92649-1030

http://www.shelleducation.com

ISBN 978-1-4258-0532-6

© *2009 Shell Education*

Made in U.S.A.

The classroom teacher may reproduce copies of materials in this book for classroom use only. The reproduction of any part for an entire school or school system is strictly prohibited. No part of this publication may be transmitted, stored, or recorded in any form without written permission from the publisher.

Table of Contents

Foreword

After a decade of increasingly intense emphasis on phonics instruction, even the researchers responsible for that turn have come to realize that it has not produced a generation of students who understand and enjoy reading, so they have turned their attention to comprehension instruction, complaining that not enough is known about "reading comprehension and thinking skills or how to address motivational...issues" (Otaiba and Torgeson 2007). Fortunately, they are wrong. It is true that not enough attention has been paid to comprehension and that research on comprehension instruction has focused rather narrowly on cognitive strategies. The greater problem, however, has been that there are few books that present a theoretically coherent yet thoroughly practical approach to comprehension instruction and thinking about text. This is where Maria Nichols's work makes a huge contribution.

Nichols's first book, *Comprehension through Conversation* (2006), was a breakthrough. It offered a practical approach to teaching comprehension that moved us beyond a simple cognitive view and it capitalized on Vygtotsky's (1978) understanding that social interactions act as scaffolds for development. It showed us how in classrooms we are nurturing not only students' thinking but also their literate minds. The transcripts of interactions among students in that book are particularly powerful. They show young students thinking together in ways rarely seen among high school students. They show students who have learned to teach themselves and one another by understanding how to talk together about books. Through other transcripts, she shows exactly how teachers have taught the students to do that.

This new book, *Talking About Text: Guiding Students to Increase Comprehension Through Purposeful Talk*, takes Nichols's groundbreaking work a step further, but more importantly, it capitalizes on her extensive experience as a literacy coach and shows step by step how to do it. She is equally clear about the how-to and the why-to, and just as in a good writing conference, she leaves us with a strong vision of what is possible for our students. She shows how, through dialogue, children come to not only comprehend better but also want to and expect to do better, as well as to enjoy the challenge of stretching themselves. She offers concise, explicit, step-by-step ways to become a master teacher of comprehension.

Although Nichols shows us how the Gradual Release of Responsibility model works in teaching comprehension, she also shows us a much less common and perhaps more important aspect of the model. There is an inherent hierarchy in the gradual release model, with the teacher holding the more powerful position. Because this relationship is part of what students learn, it is important that they also experience comprehension interactions in a more equitable way. In these situations, students learn to take control of extending their own understanding in their interactions with each other. In Nichols's classrooms, they acquire this autonomy in an engaging way and as a tool they know how to use. Students learn how to use one another to expand their own development and, in the process, learn that reading is engaging.

In the process of teaching us how to expand students' comprehension, Nichols takes us beyond comprehension to the real purpose of teaching. She shows us how teaching for comprehension simultaneously teaches for civil society: students learn to interact productively and to understand themselves and one another in new ways—ways that will lead to a peaceable classroom, and perhaps a more democratic society.

Peter H. Johnston
author of *Choice Words*

Acknowledgments

Andrew Carnegie once described teamwork as the fuel that allows common people to attain uncommon results. Thanks to colleagues who immerse themselves in their work, with curious minds and a belief that together we are capable of understanding and succeeding far better than alone, this fuel is plentiful.

My thank yous must begin with the teachers at Webster Elementary, Garfield Elementary, and numerous teachers throughout the San Diego Unified School District. Not only does their work with purposeful talk dance throughout this book, but we are privileged to peek into several of their classrooms in the pages to come.

The dynamic trio of Susie Althoff, Amy Vagdama, and Tess Suzanna—the kindergarten team at Webster Elementary—has helped me refine my understanding of students' first steps with purposeful talk. Third-grade teacher Jeralyn Treas's intuitive problem solving of difficulties with talk behavior has helped countless others support their own students through similar wobbles. I thank them for allowing me to question, hypothesize, observe, teach, and, most importantly, wonder and be amazed alongside them.

Special thanks go to Peter Johnston, Debra Crouch, Jeralyn Treas, and Chas Moriarty, who listened, read, questioned, offered feedback, listened, and read again. Their inquisitive spirit helped me define my purpose with this endeavor and maintain a clarity of message.

I'm grateful to Lori Kamola, editorial director for Shell Education, who read *Comprehension Through Conversation: The Power of Purposeful Talk in the Reading Workshop* (Nichols 2006) with the keen, practical mind of a classroom teacher. Lori looked for the beginning—the lesson design that enables first steps with purposeful talk—and smartly suggested creating it.

And lastly, I owe endless thank yous to Rick, who understands that this work is never done.

© Shell Education

Chapter 1

Introduction

"I just don't know," Katie sighed. "We've been working on talk behavior for over 10 weeks now, and I still have to remind the kids to speak to each other and not to me, and they still aren't really listening to each other—at least, not all of them. Maybe I'm doing something wrong?"

I've honestly lost count of how often I've heard variations of those same words, with the same long sigh attached each time. Teaching students to use talk purposefully in an academic setting takes time. We are teaching students to interact in extremely focused ways in an environment where many have become quite passive. We are also asking them to use this behavior in conjunction with newly learned cognitive processes, or ways of thinking, in order to better understand complex texts, ideas, and issues. This is an awe-inspiring range of considerations for students—or anyone, for that matter—to orchestrate at one time.

"Tell me about the progress your students *have* made," I encouraged, knowing full well that Katie Crommer, the classroom teacher, had much to celebrate.

"Well," Katie hesitated, eyes upward, clearly envisioning her third graders in her head. "They don't get frustrated anymore when I won't confirm whether their thoughts are right or not. They understand that they need evidence for their thinking, and they're getting that they need to talk about their ideas with each other to figure out if the thinking is on track. So their meaning making has become stronger. And some students are actually responding to what others have said when they talk, but they still look at me instead of at each other when they talk. And then there are the kids who still just sit there...."

As I listened to Katie, I knew that this was amazing progress in just 10 weeks—not only for the students, but for Katie, too. Just four months ago, when Katie and I first began working together, she was struggling with shifts in her beliefs about students' capacity for understanding, the use of talk as a tool for constructing meaning, the importance of building habits of mind, and her role in the process. Katie's evolving beliefs required her to make huge shifts in her instructional practices, such as changing her purpose and technique for questioning. Now, she encourages the exploration of ideas as opposed to quizzing for right answers, and she orchestrates talk as opposed to confirming those answers.

Like anyone who is relearning a behavior, from perfecting a golf swing to improving snacking habits, Katie experiences temporary lapses into her old practice. But not to worry—her students are developing abilities alongside her, and both she and the students are working to strengthen these abilities in surprisingly supportive ways. Just the day before, during a read-aloud, I had watched Katie excitedly yell, "Right!" after a student shared his thinking about a big idea in a text. Then, with her hand waving madly in the air as if to erase the word (and an "I know!" look shot in my direction), she regrouped and was about to ask, "What makes you think that?" But Justin beat her to the punch!

"Why do you think it's right?" he asked with a look that indicated he disagreed, but was willing to listen.

Katie smartly smiled, explained her thinking, cited evidence, and asked Justin, "What do you think?"

And isn't that just what we want? We want the students to actively seek our explanations and evidence, as well as recognize that there may be alternative possibilities as meaning is constructed. In this instance, Justin was actually taking over the role of orchestrating the talk!

Katie's developing awareness of the power of students'

purposeful talk has strengthened her ability to encourage talk, keep the talk growing, and orchestrate the talk. She simply needed to take a moment to reflect as a means of gauging clear steps for herself and the students, as opposed to being overwhelmed by the whole of the journey still ahead.

Likewise, Katie's students, as Justin so clearly illustrated, have come a very long way from the disengaged group I first observed. Many are metamorphosing into vibrant thinkers who understand that they have an active role to play in their own learning. The students are realizing the value of talk as a tool for constructing meaning, and with this realization, they are understanding the importance of considering others' thinking, listening with intent, and ultimately discovering an overall sense of power and enthusiasm for the learning process.

Is Katie doing something wrong? Absolutely not! The difficulties Katie is encountering are predictable and solvable over time. Patience—with herself and the students—mixed with high expectations—again for herself and the students—are key. In addition, the march toward success with purposeful talk requires that thoughtful lesson design be partnered with this mix of patience and high expectations—lessons that introduce and support new ways of thinking and talking together, and lessons that gradually release responsibility for the thinking and talking to the learner for the purpose of creating independent ability and habits of mind.

When I share Katie's story, the questions I am asked so often are "But how?" "How did she develop her understanding of talk?" "How did she get started?" "How did she introduce this work to her students?" "How are those lessons designed?" And the list of "how" questions keeps going and going.

This book is an attempt to answer many of these "how" questions and a few of the "what" and "why" questions that often weave their way throughout conversations about purposeful talk. As with most complex undertakings, there is no one correct, magical way to go about teaching and encouraging students to use talk as a constructivist tool. The suggestions and possible lessons you will encounter in these pages are just that—suggestions and possibilities. They are based on my experiences in my own classroom and on side-by-side coaching opportunities with remarkably dedicated teachers at a range of grade levels in schools serving varying populations of students.

Purposeful Talk: What Is It, and Why Do I Need It in My Classroom?

Two of the most common "what" and "why" questions about purposeful talk are naturally linked together into what essentially boils down to "What is purposeful talk, and why do I need it in my classroom?"

The ability of humans to think and talk together, and the end result when we do so smartly, is a focus in many arenas of our world today, with voices from the business, political, and academic sectors seeming to lead the charge. While there are differing labels for differing forms of and purposes for thinking and talking together, ways of talking that result in the co-construction of new understandings and ideas seem to take center stage.

Ralph Peterson (1992) and David Bohm (1996) make distinctions between conversation, discussion, and dialogue, pointing to dialogue as a unique way of thinking and talking together. Dialogue, Peterson asserts, is a combining of ideas that requires thoughtful listening and responding, allowing participants to collaborate and the construction of meaning to become the primary focus. David Bohm further defines dialogue as a true negotiation of meaning. In *Comprehension Through Conversation: The Power of Purposeful Talk in the Reading Workshop*, I summarize the result of successful dialogue in this way: "Through this constructive process, participants achieve a whole that is greater than the sum of its parts—ideas that are bigger and better than any individual may have conceived on their own" (Nichols 2006, 7). Because dialogue, as defined by Peterson and Bohm, is so incredibly purpose driven, I refer to this form of oral discourse as purposeful talk. Purposeful talk is focused, collaborative talk; it is a social process that requires students to actively engage with ideas, think out loud together, and work to a co-construction of those ideas. But why bring purposeful talk into the classroom? In *Classroom Discourse: The Language of Teaching and Learning*, author Courtney Cazden asserts that "the basic purpose of school is achieved through communication" (2001, 2). As Cazden points out, teachers are in charge of controlling this communication, or talk, in positive ways with the goal of enhancing learning. Research by Wolf, Crosson, and Resnick found that "effective classroom talk was linked to a high level of student's thinking and active use of knowledge" (2004). In fact, according to Simich-Dudgeon "In the last 25 years or so, research has provided significant evidence that collaborative academic talk is at the heart of the learning experience" (1998).

The Center on English Learning & Achievement (CELA), a research group affiliated with the Albany Institute for Research in Education (AIRE) in the School of Education at the University at Albany, has focused on practices that ensure that all students have the opportunity to develop the language and literacy skills necessary for success in academic settings and beyond. A report based on CELA's research on classroom discourse concludes that "learning is most effective when classrooms emphasize knowledge derived from active participation in meaningful conversations within important fields of study" (2006).

Lucy Calkins adds to this emphasis on using talk to construct understanding, concluding that "talk, like reading and writing, is a major motor—I could even say *the* major motor—of intellectual development" (2001, 226). This sentiment is echoed in the work of Lauren Resnick and the Institute for Learning at the University of Pittsburgh. In defining what she refers to as "accountable talk," Resnick argues that "talking with others about ideas and work is fundamental to learning" (1999). It seems that strong, purposeful talk is clearly linked to the depth of understanding students are able to achieve.

But this focused, purpose-driven talk does not happen by itself. In *Comprehension Through Conversation: The Power of Purposeful Talk in the Reading Workshop*, I noted that many of our students come to us knowing how to chitchat, share ideas in casual situations, tell about things, and give us reports. "But the heightened level of engagement necessary for purposeful talk may be something new to them" (Nichols 2006, 29).

Focusing on our students' abilities to use talk most often leads to the realization that all of our students need some level of support in developing and using talk purposefully. As Resnick proposes, "Teachers should intentionally create the norms and skills of accountable talk in their classrooms" (1999). And in their research of exemplary fourth-grade teachers, Richard Allington and Peter Johnston found that "not only was it [talk] modeled by the teacher in her interactions with students, but it was also deliberately taught, nurtured, and expected" (2001, 205).

Teaching students to talk purposefully necessitates the creation of emotionally and physically robust environments that encourage collaborative efforts, as well as the design of curriculum that focuses on cognitive processes that support the development of big ideas. It also requires daily lessons that focus on the combination of these cognitive processes and building purposeful talk behaviors. Yet the reality is that very little time is spent teaching students to construct meaning using talk. Lucy Calkins observes, "In schools, talk is sometimes valued and sometimes avoided, but—and this is surprising—talk is rarely taught. It is rare to hear teachers discuss their efforts to teach students to talk well" (2001, 226).

The Changing Role of the Teacher

The use of purposeful talk as a constructivist tool requires us to rethink our role in our students' learning. Constructivism values developmentally appropriate learning that is initiated and directed by the students and facilitated by the teacher. Undoubtedly, teaching was easier when having academic conversations meant asking questions that had a right answer—especially when we knew what that right answer was. Once the question was asked, the teacher simply became the judge: No… No… Not quite… You're on the right track… Yes! That's what I was looking for!

When purposeful talk is used to explore ideas, as opposed to give right answers, the teacher's role takes on new demands. The first steps begin prior to the lesson, with a mix of decisions about levels of support, thoughtful selection of texts, and backward lesson design.

During the lesson, our role becomes one of orchestration. We need to cue students to use the talk behavior they are learning to support the construction of meaning, as well as provide added support at key points in the conversation, such as clarifying, bundling ideas together, and reminding students to use specific comprehension strategies. To be successful, we must be listening closely, interpreting students' thoughts, and tracking the meaning as it builds. We speak so often about the importance of the students' level of engagement in the learning; however, when orchestrating purposeful talk, the level of the teacher's engagement matters every bit as much! As Cazden points out, "Being able to *hear* students' ideas, to understand the sense they are making, is not as easy as it may sound" (2001, 89).

After the lesson, our role is to support the students' growing abilities with thinking and talking purposefully about their thinking by debriefing and offering feedback. This enables all students to develop an understanding of the strategies and process involved in the construction of meaning and encourages them toward building habits of mind. While all this may seem daunting at first, it grows easier over time, even to the point of becoming second nature.

Defining Goals

Ultimately there are three interconnected and equally important goals for teaching purposeful talk. First we hope to build not just the ability, but also a true desire to think collaboratively with others about complex ideas and issues. This desire is derived from a history of conversations in which students were made explicitly aware of the power of thinking and talking together purposefully. While we don't always have a partner ready to discuss our thinking as we read, we hope students develop the habit of deliberately seeking out others to discuss the ideas and issues in their reading and in their world, knowing that their ideas and understandings are always strengthened by doing so. Equally as important for our students is the building of habits of mind for engaged, independent thinking, both in school and beyond. When students talk with others about their reading and thinking, they become accustomed to having their thinking questioned, having to support their thoughts with evidence, and feeling their own ideas shift and grow. Gradually students develop the understanding that there will be interpretations and points of view that differ from their own. Over time, the echoes of months and years of conversations should resound in students' minds, creating habits that guide even solo efforts. Students begin to question their own interpretations of their reading, anticipate alternative views, weigh evidence, and develop their own ideas thoughtfully so that their thinking is strong even before they engage with others. Calkins reminds us, "The great Russian psychologist Lev Vygotsky helped us realize that by giving our students practice in talking with others, we give them frames for thinking on their own" (2001, 26). John Bruer sums this up succinctly, "Discourse doesn't make thought visible, rather, thought is internalized discourse" (as cited by Cazden 2001, 75).

And with thoughtful lesson design that moves students' thinking and talking beyond the text, we hope students will develop the habit of using their constructed understandings of texts and ideas to better understand and engage with their world, questioning, hypothesizing, and acting upon it in positive ways. In this way, purposeful talk becomes a tool for understanding and successfully navigating the possibilities and challenges of the twenty-first century.

Navigating This Book

The ideas and possible lessons you will find in these pages will help you take the first steps with purposeful talk and work toward developing your students' independence with thinking and talking about ideas.

In Chapter 1: Introduction, we focus on the major "what" and "why" questions surrounding purposeful talk. Purposeful talk is defined, and a rationale for teaching purposeful talk is discussed. Now we need to get busy!

As we move on to Chapter 2: Getting the Talk Started: Lessons That Teach Purposeful Talk Behavior, we will continue addressing "what" questions about purposeful talk by taking a more detailed look at the body of behaviors that enable students to use talk constructively. Then we begin answering the "how" questions by considering highly supported lessons that teach beginning talk behavior. To bring the lessons to life, they are embedded in actual classrooms at a variety of grade levels and at various stages of the progression of purposeful talk. The lessons are designed to focus on both the cognitive processes students need in order to build their comprehension abilities and the talk behavior that helps them deepen their thinking. The supporting information will also help you consider what adjustments to the lessons may be necessary to suit your students' unique needs.

From there, Chapter 3: Creating Habits of Mind: Lessons That Teach Students to Read, Think, and Talk Independently will continue our in-depth consideration of "how" questions. This section focuses on lesson design that builds independence with specific ways of thinking about nonfiction reading using the gradual release of responsibility model. We will track the work from Chapter 1 in one of our classrooms as a variety of instructional approaches and supports are used to release responsibility to the students for thinking and talking together.

Chapter 4: Maintaining the Momentum with Purposeful Talk will offer suggestions for working through difficulties with purposeful talk. As Katie has discovered, developing the ability to talk purposefully in an academic setting is challenging for the teacher and students alike. This section is intended to not only serve as a wealth of suggestions for bumps in the road, but also to create comfort in the realization that difficulties with talk are predictable and solvable. It also reminds us that strong purposeful talk requires constant vigilance.

And lastly, Chapter 5: What Can Be will leave us with a vision of possibility—a glimpse of students developing an awareness of the power of purposeful talk, of the depth of understanding they are capable of constructing when they think and talk together, and of their abilities to draw on these understandings in order to re-create their world.

Getting the Talk Started: Lessons That Teach Purposeful Talk Behavior

Clarisse: *I know that's like, how the mom is, 'cause my mom, she does that all the time—like the mom in the book. She gets really mad, 'cause when I spill stuff…*

Tyrell: *What is it?*

Clarisse: *That spilled? Just like her (pointing to a picture of a young girl and spilled juice dripping off a kitchen table in the read-aloud text being held by the teacher). Juice—all ooooverrrr the floor.*

Roberto: *Me, too—I did that, and my Dad told me I hafta go outside…*

Clarisse: *My mom was really mad 'cause I spill all the time.*

Roberto: *…and he says I gotta clean it up…*

Jazmine: *Once, I spilled my cereal—it was the Sponge Bob kind, and my dog got it…*

Daniel: *Hey, that's like me! Once, me and my brother, we were eating that kind, and the milk knocked over.*

This delightful chat, buoyed with boasts of clumsiness and parental disapproval, erupted during a read-aloud of *Harriet, You'll Drive Me Wild!* by Mem Fox (2000). This amusing story about the depth of maternal love, told through the exploits of Harriet, a naughty little girl who pushes the limits of her mother's patience, clearly cut close to home for many of these second graders. The students' talk, precipitated by several pages of Harriet's childhood antics, was lively and animated, with each student involved firmly convinced that they alone owned the title of master spiller.

But let's delve a little deeper. I used the term *chat* for this exchange intentionally. Although these five students seemed comfortable talking, the talk lacked purpose beyond the sharing of their experiences and the amusement of others. There was no development of ideas and no use of talk to delve into the deeper meaning in the text or transfer that thinking to understandings of our world.

As I listened, I noted that while the students were definitely connecting to the text, their connections were at the literal level. I wondered if the students were aware of when (or if) their connections were supporting them in constructing a stronger understanding of this text and when the connections were pulling them into their own narratives, leaving the text far behind.

And it's curious that in a class of 20 students, only five burst out with stories to document the chaos of spilling accidents, a common childhood occurrence. Even I was twinging with flashes of my own classic red-wine-on-the-carpet mishap just the weekend before.

Where were the other voices? Did the silent majority in this class have rich thoughts in their heads? Were they constructing meaning? Many were grinning, obviously finding delight in the confessions of their peers. Some even scooted in on their knees to hear and gain a better visual of the speaker. What was keeping them from joining in on the "once I spilled" extravaganza?

And what of the handful of students who were not only silent, but clearly disengaged? Not a smile, not a glance at the speaker, not a glimmer of a thought or a hint of the construction of meaning crossed their motionless faces. What do these students believe learning to be, and what is their understanding of their roles in the process?

This snapshot of collective-engagement behaviors is not out of the ordinary. In fact, the scenario may feel somewhat familiar. In classrooms where students are encouraged to talk but have not yet explored the use of purposeful talk, we generally find variations of this same mix—students who share their thinking readily and easily (whether it supports meaning making or not), those who monitor the exchanges, hovering on the edge, and those who choose to disengage.

The remainder of Chapters 2 and 3 will focus on the design of daily lessons for all of these students—lessons that encourage them to think in specific ways about their reading and use talk as a tool for constructing meaning, with the goal of deep comprehension of texts and critical understandings about their world.

Building Beginning Talk Behavior

The range of behaviors students need to develop as they learn to use talk as a tool can and should be directly taught and strengthened over time (see the following section, Purposeful Talk Behaviors). While there is not necessarily a hierarchy to these behaviors, it is safe to say that developing an ability to hear all voices, to add to the talk in meaningful ways, and to listen with intent significantly supports the students' abilities to keep lines of thinking alive, resulting in stronger negotiation of meaning. That said, it makes sense to focus first on hearing all voices and adding to the talk in meaningful ways, and then teaching students to listen with intent for the purpose of keeping lines of thinking alive before launching into negotiating meaning.

Purposeful Talk Behaviors (Nichols 2006, 41–47)

Hearing all voices

For ideas to grow to their fullest potential, and for all students to develop the necessary habits of mind, we need to be sure that every student understands his or her role as an active, engaged learner. This means all learners are thinking and sharing their thinking with others by talking.

Saying something meaningful

Once all students are engaged in the ongoing conversations—either sharing their thinking with the whole group or at least with a partner during a *turn and talk* (see pages 26 and 27 for a detailed explanation of a turn and talk)—we up the ante and develop their abilities to consider the power of their thinking as it relates to the construction of meaning. Students need to learn how to differentiate between loose associations and thoughts that support deeper understanding.

Listening with intent

The dynamic listening required to grasp another person's idea, fully consider it, and actively respond may be unfamiliar behavior for many of our students. Learning to listen purposefully is a crucial step in the process of learning to talk purposefully.

Keeping lines of thinking alive

Once students are listening with intent, they are better able to stay focused on single ideas, using talk purposefully to build these ideas to their fullest potential. As students learn to keep the talk focused, they also learn how to hold onto thoughts that would potentially move the talk in another direction while an idea is being pursued.

Negotiating meaning

As students pursue ideas together, there will naturally be differences of opinion. Students need to learn how to struggle with thinking that might not immediately make sense to them, give ideas a chance even if they don't immediately agree, and be flexible with their own thinking. Learning to disagree with respect is a crucial piece of this process.

———◆———

This entire range of purposeful talk behaviors should be taught to students of all grade levels. Ideally, school sites will focus on this work collectively so that aside from the launch year, each progressive grade is strengthening students' abilities to use talk as a tool for constructing meaning as opposed to teaching the behaviors from scratch. This building upon the use of talk in previous grades is crucial, as it goes without saying that students will have a greater capacity to keep a line of thinking alive in third grade than in kindergarten, or that a negotiation of meaning will have a far greater depth and level of intensity in a sixth-grade classroom than in a first-grade classroom. A continual focus on talk behavior as it is used to understand increasingly complex texts and ideas year upon year is what encourages the formation of habits of mind.

The lessons that follow will be situated in classrooms for the purpose of bringing the lessons to life. These classrooms contain a mix of students who are strengthening purposeful talk behavior and students who are just now learning purposeful talk behavior because of a variety of factors, including high transiency rates at the school sites.

Determining the Lesson Focus

While the lessons that follow are designed with a dual focus on cognitive processes and talk, it is important to note that teachers embarking on instruction in purposeful talk behavior do have the option of designing lessons that focus on talk behaviors alone. If the choice is made to offer lessons that focus only on talk behavior, it is essential that the lessons be designed to result in the authentic construction of meaning, as opposed to practicing isolated behaviors with no clear-cut purpose. The key to helping students understand the potential for purposeful talk is texts that are sure to generate excitement through compelling themes. The texts must also be accessible to the students through the combination of talk and cognitive processes the students already control.

Some primary teachers whose students are new to purposeful talk have discovered success with designing a brief mini-lesson to practice the talk behaviors and then immediately embedding the behaviors in lessons where they are used in conjunction with a cognitive process focus for the purpose of constructing meaning. These mini-lessons offer explicit instruction in a specific talk behavior, a quick try of the behavior with a simple talk topic, and an equally quick debrief with teacher feedback before drawing on the talk behavior for a more complex purpose. In some kindergarten classrooms, these mini-lessons teach behaviors as simple as how to turn knee to knee with your partner and then turn back to the whole class.

When it comes to deciding whether to offer separate lessons designed to build comfort with talk behavior or embed the learning of talk behavior into lessons designed to keep ongoing work around cognitive processes moving forward, there is not necessarily a clear-cut, right way to go. The decision often depends on the complexity of the ongoing work, students' progress with work to that point in time, and their current abilities to talk together for the purpose of constructing meaning. Take comfort in knowing that whichever decision is made, it is not a final decision. If instruction in using purposeful talk is embedded in lessons with a cognitive process focus and the demand of the two combined proves too challenging at first, there is always the option of stepping back and building some ability with purposeful talk separately. Once students reach a comfort level with the talk behaviors, lessons can be designed that re-engage the students with the new cognitive processes and draw on their abilities with talk for the purpose of constructing meaning.

Lesson Design

All of the lessons that follow document real work with purposeful talk from classrooms that I have been privileged to work in with varying degrees of intensity. Before delving into the lessons, it is important to take a moment here to state the obvious. None of the classrooms highlighted in these lessons is your classroom, and none of the students for whom these lessons were designed are your students. The hope is that you will not focus on each lesson as an absolute, but rather draw out its essence and refine the design so it meets the unique needs of the group of students you are guiding each day.

The classrooms showcased in each lesson are in elementary schools in lower socioeconomic urban neighborhoods. While the exact makeup of the classrooms varies from room to room and site to site, all are ethnically diverse and have significant numbers of English language learners.

Each lesson is designed with a dual focus: a purposeful talk focus and a cognitive process focus. The students are reminded of both focuses in the lesson introduction so that they are prepared to think in specific ways and talk about their thinking purposefully.

Equally important, the debrief at the end of each lesson is conducted through the lens of both focuses. During the lesson debrief, the teacher explains that thinking about the text in a particular way, and talking about that thinking purposefully, enabled the construction of meaning. Bruer shares, "Social interactions…allow skilled thinkers to demonstrate expert strategies to the naïve…[It] makes hidden thought processes public and shared (as cited by Cazden 2001, 75).

It is important to note that these debriefs cannot be planned in detail prior to the lesson, as a strong debrief draws from specifics that unfold as the lesson progresses. Each lesson plan includes general language for the debrief, which needs to be bolstered by examples from your students' own thinking and talking.

The cognitive process focus for each lesson is drawn from the standards-based curriculum for that particular grade level. Each lesson should be considered as one of a string of lessons that build students' abilities to think and talk in specific ways inside a particular unit of study.

The particular talk focus of each lesson is simply a matter of the progression of the students' developing abilities with talk and the behaviors needed at that point in order to continue to construct understanding. Clearly, a single lesson will not enable students to gain enough experience with the talk focus to use it successfully and develop independence. Again, each lesson should be considered as one in a string of lessons that will focus on the necessary talk behavior.

The grade level of the classroom used to bring each lesson to life is not intended to suggest an ideal grade level for introducing the specific talk behavior(s). Again, the full combination of talk behaviors should be taught to students of all grade levels who are new to talk and strengthened in students who are experienced in using talk as a tool for constructing meaning. Teachers at varying grade levels will need to use their own judgment as they read, think, and talk about these lessons. This may involve changing the text, adapting the pace of the lesson, lessening or increasing the amount of support, and adjusting the complexity of their language to meet the needs and abilities of their own students.

In designing these lessons, the stopping places and the way talk is initiated and supported require a great deal of thought. Ideally, we want to stop often enough to discuss any information that is crucial for the ongoing construction of meaning and offers the opportunity to think and talk through the lens of the cognitive process focus. What we don't want to do is stop to talk so often that meaning is lost, or create an artificial pattern for stopping—every page, every two pages, every paragraph. This leads students to believe that knowing where to pause to think and talk when reading independently is about the amount of text rather than the density of information or ideas. That's not to say that we never stop at the end of every page or every paragraph. It simply depends on the text formatting and the author's way of presenting information.

In many of the lessons that follow, students are offered the opportunity to turn and talk to a partner. A *turn and talk* is simply an opportunity to quickly turn to a partner and discuss ideas or confusions during a lesson. The reasons for a turn and talk will vary. Often it is used so that all students have the opportunity to have their voices heard. Some students need the support of a turn and talk to clarify thinking and/or translate their thoughts to English. When the ideas in the text are complex, a turn and talk offers an opportunity to think together with a partner prior to sharing a thought with the whole class. During a turn and talk, teachers will peruse the pairs of students as they talk, listening in order to gauge the use of talk itself, the use of the cognitive processes on which the lesson focuses, and the construction of meaning. He or she may pause and offer support to specific partnerships as well. After a minute or two, students are drawn back to the whole group, and either the floor is opened to anyone who wants to initiate whole-group conversation or specific individuals are asked to launch the talk.

Turn-and-talk partnerships work best when the decisions of whom to pair together are purposeful. What is most important is that the partners are able to think together without one partner dominating the other. Shy students, or those who need language support, may require partners who are able to coax and coach without doing the work for them.

Many of the lessons make reference to posters that are being, or already have been, co-created by the students and teacher. These posters are created for the purpose of supporting students as they read, think, and talk with increasing amounts of independence. Classrooms in which purposeful talk thrives are filled with posters and charts that support both the thinking work, or cognitive processes, and talk behaviors.

An important last note on lesson design: the greater the students' depth of thinking and talking about their ideas, the longer the read-aloud lessons become. It is beneficial to fall into the habit of planning possible stopping places in the anticipated flow of conversation and the construction of meaning, just in case time dictates that the lesson be continued the following day.

Using the Lessons

Each of the lessons in this chapter is surrounded by supporting information, beginning with the specific talk behavior(s) the lesson is designed to address. This is followed by context—a sense of the classroom being used as a backdrop for the lesson. The classroom context will include the reason for the specific talk-behavior focus, as well as the cognitive process focus that the lesson is also designed to address. This information will help you understand decisions in the lesson design and the teacher's in-the-moment decision making in the narrative that follows.

Next, you will find the actual lesson plan. The lesson design begins with both the cognitive process focus and the purposeful talk focus, and the meaning that students are thinking and talking toward during the lesson. It is crucial to note that the idea jotted in this cell is only one possible interpretation or direction that the thinking and talking might take. Rich texts dance around many complex issues from the world, and we need to be accepting of other possibilities that may develop as the thinking and talking builds—including those we hadn't considered ourselves—so that the lesson does not become a "right answer" exercise. Next you will notice cells for Text, Goal, and Introduction.

The lesson plan continues with five columns intended to guide your progression through the lesson. The first column offers suggested stopping places to allow thinking time and encourage talk. The second column suggests questions that might be used to kick off the talk, beginning with an open-ended "What are you thinking?" gradually followed by more supportive questions. This open-ended choice allows us to determine whether students are thinking through the lens of the cognitive process focus before we begin to prompt for it. The students in these lessons are used to this question and generally respond smartly to it. However, the question could confuse students who simply aren't used to being asked what they are thinking!

The third column helps us consider the talk we would like to hear from our students—talk indicative of strong meaning making at that particular point in the text. The fourth column lists possible talk difficulties we should be prepared for, while the last column offers suggestions for supporting the students if talk does not develop. These suggestions may include model thinking, rereading of the text, more detailed questioning, or reminding the students to draw on specific cognitive processes. Below the columns you will find space to write in the following sections: Process Debrief, Meaning Debrief, and Notes and Reflection. A blank copy of the lesson plan form is included in Appendix A for classroom use.

Following each lesson plan is a narrative of the lesson, which allows you to "see" a segment of the lesson unfold. Each narrative includes a partial transcript chosen because it clearly illustrates the teacher's efforts to support the students in using the combination of specific cognitive processes and talk behavior for the purpose of constructing meaning.

And most importantly, the last segment will deconstruct the lesson through the lens of the focus questions on the following page. This information will enable you to focus in on crucial aspects of each lesson, facilitating careful consideration of decisions the teacher made as he or she worked to orchestrate the talk. As you read this section, keep your students in the forefront of your mind, reflecting on their strengths and needs as thinkers, talkers, and meaning makers. This will help you think about the in-the-moment decisions you will need to make as you work to orchestrate talk in your own classroom.

Focus Questions for Deconstructing Lessons

- **How does the lesson design balance the focus on talk with the focus on cognitive processes?**

  Students need to develop an understanding of where readers stop and think using the cognitive processes and how talk strengthens this thinking. In addition, talk should be used to make visible the way thinking builds throughout and beyond the text to make meaning.

- **How does the teacher step in and out of the conversation to teach the use of purposeful talk without interrupting the construction of meaning?**

  Teachers take an active role in orchestrating purposeful talk. We must offer enough support to teach students to use their talk purposefully and shape the conversation, but do so without interruption to the point that we interfere with the students' construction of meaning.

- **How is responsibility for purposeful talk behaviors transferred to the students?**

  During the progression of each lesson and across lessons, teachers will need to gradually release responsibility for the use of the cognitive processes and the talk behavior to the students, lessening or increasing support as necessary.

- **How are students made aware of the link between cognitive processes, purposeful talk behavior, and the construction of meaning?**

  During and after each lesson, the teacher should clearly delineate this relationship. Talk should develop an awareness of the range of possible responses to texts, broadening perspectives and developing the capacity to think critically on their own. This helps students value purposeful talk and strategic thinking, as well as shape new habits of mind.

Lesson 1

Purposeful Talk Behavior: Hearing All Voices

As early as possible in their academic careers, students need to understand that learning is an active endeavor. Setting the expectation that all are engaged and thinking during learning opportunities and will share that thinking with others is a crucial step in developing this awareness.

When students trust their peers and know that they will be supported in their efforts to articulate their thinking, they will begin to grow in their abilities to add their voices to ongoing conversations. Turn and talks are often used for support in this process. Although brief, the time with a partner gives students the opportunity to think out loud, clarify confusions, develop and articulate an idea, and gain support in translating their thinking into English.

It is vital that whenever the class pauses to think and talk together, the teacher monitors in order to be certain that a variety of voices is heard during whole-group discussion, and that all students are sharing their thinking during the turn and talks. The latter may require the teacher to move around the circle, checking in with partnerships and providing support if necessary. This checking-in process will also enable the teacher to entice those who haven't yet shared their thinking with the whole group to do so and also make sure that ideas with the potential to strengthen meaning making are shared with the whole group.

Classroom Context

The kindergartners in this scenario are in their third week of school. Like all kindergartners early in the year, they are just coming to grips with their new surroundings, daily routines, and the intellectual demands of the classroom.

The students have already engaged in a series of mini-lessons, as discussed earlier in this section, focused on teaching the importance of hearing all voices. In these mini-lessons, the students learned to turn to a partner, share their thinking, and ask their partner what he or she is thinking, all for the purpose of learning about each other. A purposeful-talk chart was developed by the teacher during this process, with reminders to sit knee-to-knee, make eye contact, and take turns talking. The teacher drew visual icons to go along with each of these rules to help students remember them.

This lesson was a first experience in embedding this talk behavior into a read-aloud in order to construct meaning. Their teacher, Sara Kingston, chose a text that the students would easily connect to, because in addition to developing their talk behavior, she wanted them to develop the understanding that making and using connections enable readers to construct deeper meaning. Sara's text choice was a level A book from the *Explorations* series. The text, *Playing Outside* (Woolley 2003), features beautiful photographs of smiling children playing outside together, including kite flying, riding bikes, and other games most students know well.

On the following two pages you will see a lesson plan for Lesson 1. Following the lesson plan you will find the lesson narrative. Then you will come to a section titled Deconstructing the Lesson.

Lesson Plan—Teaching Purposeful Talk Behavior to Support the Construction of Meaning

Cognitive Process Focus: *(This is the way(s) of thinking and talking about reading that the students are learning in order to support the construction of meaning.)*

using our own lives to help us construct meaning

Text: *Playing Outside* by Marilyn Woolley (Explorations)

Introduction: *(Include the cognitive process focus, the talk behavior that will be used to develop ideas, and text introduction.)*

Today we're going to read a book about something fun and familiar to all of you. The book is called *Playing Outside* by Marilyn Woolley. As we read, we're going to think about ourselves and how we are like the children in this text. Thinking about ourselves

Stopping place	Cue for getting the talk started	Desired-response possibilities
cover and title (to predict and generate connections)	What do you see on the cover? What do you expect we'll read about inside?	The kids are playing on the swing. It will be about games you play outside, like…
Page 5 (to begin to link the use of connections, talking about ideas, and meaning making)	What games are the children playing? Why are they playing together? How do you know?	All the kids are playing together. It's more fun than playing alone. I know because when I play…
Page 11 (to deepen the link between the use of connections, talking about ideas, and meaning making)	Are the children still playing together and having fun? How does this make playing better?	These friends do a lot of different things. When I play like this with my friends…
the end (to deepen the link between the use of connections, talking about ideas, and meaning making)	Do the moms make it more fun? How do you know?	When my mom plays with me and my friends, it's the best because…

Process Debrief: *(State the cognitive processes and talk behavior that enabled the construction of meaning.)*

We were able to construct this meaning because you thought very hard about your own life—how you love playing games with friends—and used that thinking to give you ideas about this book. All of you shared your ideas with your partners, and some of you shared them with the whole class. This smart thinking and talking helped us understand the students in this book.

Purposeful Talk Focus: *(This is the talk behavior the students are focused on in support of the construction of meaning.)*
hearing all voices

Goal: *(This is the meaning that students are thinking and talking toward.)*
Being with friends makes playing more fun (one of many possible themes).

Introduction *(cont.):* will help us understand what we read even better. Remember, everyone needs to be ready to talk and share his or her ideas. You'll have a chance to turn and talk with a partner, and then we'll share our thinking.

Anticipating talk difficulties	Support if necessary
• Shyness • Support with vocabulary for games (flying kites, yo-yo…) • Students telling their own stories about playing and forgetting to give their partner a chance to talk	Model think-aloud: I'm seeing two children playing together outside on the swings. What fun! What other fun ways to play together outside do you think the author will tell us about?
	Model think-aloud: What fun games! All of the children are playing with friends. I know that when I play with friends, I have more fun because we laugh a lot… Thinking about myself is helping me to…
	These children must like playing together because they are doing so many different things. When I'm having fun, I like to keep playing just as they are…
	I remember when my mom used to play with me my friends and me… Thinking about myself is really helping me…

Meaning Debrief: *(This is the meaning that students constructed.)*
We think this text is really about the way friends make playing so much more fun. We thought about the friends in our lives and how much we enjoy them (one of many possible conclusions).

Notes and Reflection: *(State observations that help with the design of future lessons, text selection, small-group support, and/or individual student support. Notes may include thoughts on the level of support with either the cognitive processes or talk behavior, strength of the text selection, lesson length, etc.)*
- Many students still need turn and talk to share their ideas.
- Some students are ready to enter conversation without a turn and talk.
- Most students readily connected to the characters in this text and are ready for a slightly more difficult text.
- Some students need more work on connecting with supportive text.

Lesson Narrative

As suspected, these kindergarten students readily connected to the idea of playing with friends, and most had plenty to say. When the class stopped to construct meaning after page 5 in the book, Sara cued the students to use both their connections and talk to understand the children in the text.

Ms. Kingston: *Why are the children playing together? Turn to your partner and talk. Remember, think about yourself to help you (cognitive process focus). Each of you needs to take a turn sharing your thinking (purposeful talk focus).*

Each student turned to his or her partner, some with gentle nudging from the teacher, and began talking. The teacher moved from partnership to partnership, prompting and supporting as necessary. After listening to several partnerships, she decided to begin the whole-class conversation with Tyler and Devin.

Ms. Kingston: *Turn your bodies back to the circle. (This required a little teacher support.) I heard everyone talking to their partners and sharing their ideas to help them understand the children in the text. Tyler, what were you and your partner saying?*

Tyler: *He (pointing to his partner) said it's fun.*

Devin: *Yeah—that (pointing to the photograph of children kicking balls). It is! You hafta have somebody kick it back. And you gotta go get it!*

Ms. Kingston: *So playing with friends is fun? Do the rest of you agree?*

All students: *Yes!*

Ms. Kingston: *Kayla, that's what you and Austin were talking about, too! What were you saying? (Prompting Kayla was a purposeful move on the teacher's part. Kayla was shy, but had been getting braver about talking in a whole-group situation.)*

Kayla:	'Cause I play—and my friends play with me. I like it.
Austin:	And me, too (shaking head vigorously)—if my friends play with me.
Jinelle:	We like to play, and them, too (pointing to the children in the book).
Miguel:	She's smiling (pointing to the photograph of a girl holding the ball and grinning joyously)!
Ms. Kingston:	Does playing with a friend make you happy? (Yeses and head nodding from the students.) Ask your partner, does playing with a friend make you happy?

The students turn to their partners, ask the question, and swap answers, again with some teacher support.

Ms. Kingston:	Do you think these children are happy, just like you when you play with friends? (Yeses and head nodding again.) So you used what you know about yourself to understand the children in the book (cognitive process focus). Hearing ideas from so many of you is helping us understand (purposeful talk focus). Let's keep reading and thinking.

Remembering that some students needed support with their turn and talks when the class paused to talk after page 5, Sara took a moment before the pause after page 11 to remind them how to turn to their partners on their own and start talking. "Use the chart to help you remember," she coaxed (chart description is on page 31).

At the end of the lesson, Sara tied the work together by making the students' process visible. She closed by reminding the students that when they read, they should always use what they know about themselves to think and talk about their ideas.

Deconstructing the Lesson

So what is the next step? The obvious answer is more of the same, with both the cognitive process focus and the purposeful talk focus. The students need many lessons with texts they readily connect to, and eventually texts in which the connections require more effort, to understand the power of connections as a means of constructing meaning. Likewise, they need to continue focusing on hearing all voices until they all turn easily to partners and begin to talk without support, share their thinking in whole-group discussions with greater ease, and understand that doing so strengthens everyone's understanding.

- **How does the lesson design balance the focus on talk with the focus on cognitive processes?**

  This lesson focused on both a fairly new talk behavior and a new cognitive process (making connections). As these are beginning-of-the-year kindergartners, the questions that prompted the thinking and talking were very supportive. The students were asked to turn and talk with their partners during each stopping place to discuss ideas prompted by the questions. This was partially because so many of the kindergartners in this class do not yet have the confidence to speak out in the whole group without the support of a turn and talk, and partially because a partner talk would help the students think through their connections before talking together, allowing for more talk in general.

- **How does the teacher step in and out of the conversation to teach the use of purposeful talk without interrupting the construction of meaning?**

  Sara orchestrated each turn and talk and the building of whole-group talk by asking questions, highlighting important ideas, and encouraging students to talk more. She supported the construction of meaning by choosing those students who had strong thoughts or connections to share their thinking with the others, and then summing up the thinking. This is highly supportive, which is quite necessary in most beginning-of-the-year kindergarten classrooms.

- **How is responsibility for purposeful talk behaviors transferred to the students?**

  After realizing during the pause at page 5 that she needed to support several students in turning quickly to their partners and beginning to talk, Sara had the students take a moment to think through their talk behavior prior to talking after page 11. The students were reminded to use a classroom poster for support. This helped many more of the students turn and talk without the teacher's help.

- **How are the students made aware of the link between cognitive processes, purposeful talk behavior, and the construction of meaning?**

  After the conversation at each stopping place, Sara summed up the thinking and pointed out the way that making connections (the cognitive process focus) and hearing ideas from everyone (the purposeful talk focus) lead to the construction of meaning. After debriefing the meaning that the students constructed, she highlighted the way that thinking smartly and talking about the thinking made the meaning stronger.

Lesson 2

Purposeful Talk Behavior: Say Something Meaningful

When engaging texts and stimulating ideas get students' minds humming, they tend to share whatever pops into their heads, especially when they know the expectation is that they will talk about their thinking. As our students become adept at sharing their thinking, they need to learn to judge the relevance and power of their thoughts, the relevance to the idea being developed, and the power to build stronger ideas. At this point, we stop students whose ideas are disconnected or moving the talk in a direction that will not enable the construction of meaning and ask them to consider whether their ideas are helping to make meaning of this particular text. In classrooms with positive, supportive emotional environments, this feedback is easily accepted, and eventually the students prove remarkably adept at learning to make the determination for themselves.

Classroom Context

We opened Chapter 2 by eavesdropping on thoughts that popped into a group of second-graders' heads during a read-aloud of Mem Fox's *Harriet, You'll Drive Me Wild!* (2000). The students in this class are into their fourth week of school and up to this point had been focusing on hearing all voices. As evidenced by what they said, a handful of students need to continue with this focus and will do so in small-group instruction.

As for the others, although many of the students still need the support of a turn and talk to get the talk started, the majority are willing to talk with their partners and share with the whole group when invited to do so. However, the students were in the habit of sharing whatever popped into their heads, whether it furthered the construction of meaning or not. Sylvia Ramirez, the classroom teacher, and I felt the students needed to focus on considering the power of their ideas and monitoring themselves to be sure they were saying something that supports meaning making.

This talk work was embedded into the third of a progression of instructional opportunities designed around a cognitive process focus: learning to infer what is in a character's heart by considering what the character does, says, and thinks. The text *Harriet, You'll Drive Me Wild!* was chosen for this lesson because we suspected the students would be capable of not only drawing from their experiences with naughty behavior and frazzled parents—which we suspected would bubble up in their talk—but using what Harriet and her mother say, do, and think to make meaning.

On the following two pages you will see a lesson plan for Lesson 2. Following the lesson plan you will find the lesson narrative. Then you will come to a section titled Deconstructing the Lesson.

Lesson Plan—Teaching Purposeful Talk Behavior to Support the Construction of Meaning

Cognitive Process Focus: *(This is the way(s) of thinking and talking about reading that the students are learning in order to support the construction of meaning.)*
using what characters do, say, and think to understand what is in their hearts

Text: *Harriet, You'll Drive Me Wild!* by Mem Fox

Introduction: *(Include the cognitive process focus, the talk behavior that will be used to develop ideas, and text introduction.)*
We've been studying the way that thinking about what a character does, says, and thinks can help us understand what is in a character's heart. Yesterday we found that studying Franklin's actions—what he did—helped us understand that he felt bad about being mean to his friends. We added this thinking to our chart. Today we're going to read *Harriet, You'll Drive Me Wild!* by Mem Fox, and think and talk to understand these characters. When we think about a text, lots of ideas pop into our heads. Some of those ideas

Stopping place	Cue for getting the talk started	Desired-response possibilities
the page after Harriet dribbles jam (to begin developing a sense of Harriet)	What are you thinking? What does this tell you about Harriet?	First she spilled the juice, then the jam. She's supposed to be careful. I bet she'll feel bad—but she didn't mean to do that. Kids spill sometimes.
the page after Harriet slides off her chair (to further build an understanding of Harriet and begin to understand Mom)	What are you thinking? What do Harriet's actions tell you? What's going on with Mom? Do her words and actions help you know what's in her heart?	Harriet is really being bad. I can tell because of the things she does, such as, she keeps making bigger and bigger messes. Her mom wasn't mad before, but she's really getting mad now. I can tell because of the way she stands and what she says. I don't think Harriet's really sorry, though—she looks mad, too.
"There was a terrible silence." (to predict based on what we know about Mom)	What are you thinking? What will happen this time? Mom was getting mad before. I wonder how she will feel now.	Oh no! Now she's done it. Mom will be furious! She's been nice up to now, but this is really bad! I'm not sure Mom will say nice things this time.
the end	What are you thinking? What happened with Mom? Why did she get mad, then hug Harriet, and finally end up laughing? Do you think Harriet's behavior will change now? Is this how real Moms behave? How does thinking about this help us?	I can tell Harriet really did feel sorry because she cried. Her mom got really mad. I could tell because of the look on her face, and she yelled. But she still loves her. You can tell because she hugs her, and they clean up together. Mom just lost her patience. After she yelled, she felt sorry. My mom is like that, too. I think that when I get in trouble, I should think about how my mom feels, and…

Process Debrief: *(State the cognitive processes and talk behavior that enabled the construction of meaning.)*
Today we really worked on making sure that the ideas that popped into our heads were helping us understand the story. When ideas took our thinking in the wrong direction, we parked them on the side of our brains and got back to thinking about the text. When we thought about ideas that helped us focus more closely on the text, we realized they helped us notice more about what the characters were saying, doing, and thinking. When we talked about this, it really helped us understand Harriet's mom.

Purposeful Talk Focus: *(This is the talk behavior the students are focused on in support of the construction of meaning.)*
say something meaningful

Goal: *(This is the meaning that students are thinking and talking toward.)*
Even though we may get frustrated with those we love, we don't stop loving them (one of many possible big ideas.)

Introduction *(cont.)*: help us understand the text better, but other ideas distract us. They make us think about other things. Today we're also going to decide whether what we're thinking and saying actually helps us understand better. If it isn't, we're going to learn to park, or stop, the thinking that gets in the way and focus our brain on ideas that help—and then talk about those ideas.

Anticipating talk difficulties	Support if necessary
• Students who need the support of a turn and talk • Students' connections taking them off into their own narratives instead of propelling them deeper into the text	Wow—she spilled juice, then jam. Let's go back and look again. I'm wondering if it was on purpose or an accident. How would you describe Harriet's behavior? What kind of a student is she?
	On every page, Harriet is doing something wrong. Her mom doesn't seem as calm anymore. Let's go back to the page after Harriet spills the paint. Look closely at Mom. Just look at what Mom and Harriet are doing. What can you tell just from this? Listen to Mom's words again (reread page). What are you thinking?
	I'm looking behind Mom at Harriet and the mess she made. We know Mom has slowly been getting angry with Harriet. I also know that at some point, moms might lose their temper. What do you think?
	I know that sometimes when I'm pushed too far, I get mad. But then I feel sorry afterward. Could that have happened here? How do you know? What does this tell you about Mom?

Meaning Debrief: (This is the meaning that students constructed.)

We think this text is really about the love of special people in our lives. We realized that these people always love us, even if they get mad at us. This made us think about their feelings, and how we can be more understanding (one of many possibilities)

Notes and Reflection: *(State observations that help with the design of future lessons, text selection, small-group support, and/or individual student support.)*

• The text was too challenging for some students. I need to rethink the selection for tomorrow's lesson.

• The students' ideas are still loosely connected. They need to work on pushing towards deeper meaning.

Lesson Narrative

Let's pick up the conversation after the second pause in the lesson design.

Ms. Ramirez: *I still hear just a few of you sharing stories. Quickly, everybody turn and talk to your partners. But as you're talking, I want you to think—how do the ideas popping into your head help you understand this story? Are you ready, Jonathan (one of the students who appeared to be disengaged)?*

Jonathan nods, and the students turn immediately to their partners, the hum of voices filling the classroom. The teacher listens in to the partnerships, making sure that Jonathan and the other previously silent students are talking. Then she pauses with Jazmine and her partner. Jazmine is still talking about her dog.

Ms. Ramirez: *Jazmine, I hear you telling about something very funny. I know the book made this pop into your head, but I'm wondering, is it helping you understand this story or keeping you from thinking about the story?*

Jazmine flashes a "you caught me grin," turns to her partner and asks him what he thinks.

Next, Sylvia moves on to Clarisse and her partner, Jesse. Clarisse is continuing to tell her spilled-juice story with great detail and drama, moving the partnership further and further from the text. Sylvia points this out, asking Clarisse to think about her ideas and try to use them to say something that will help them understand the text. Clarisse looks at Sylvia, clearly puzzled.

Ms. Ramirez: *Does Harriet's mom react the same way as your mom?*

Clarisse: *Nooooo! (Shaking her head vigorously for added emphasis.) Her mom doesn't get mad.*

Jesse: *Her mom's different. Mine, too.*

Sylvia listens in, then calls the class back together and asks Clarisse and Jesse to start off the talk.

Clarisse: *We were all talking about how our moms get mad. Well, but she (Harriet's mom) didn't—until this page. But she isn't really, really mad.*

Jesse: *Yeah, her mom's really different.*

Alejandra: *Oh! She's nice.*

Ms. Ramirez: *How do you know?*

Lisette: *It's 'cause of the picture—the other one—go back... yeah, that one! See, the mom, she hugs her, and she's on her lap.*

David: *Yeah—and she said nice stuff. She didn't yell. So she's not a...a...she's not mad or nothing.*

Shandra: *It's like she (the mom) gets that she's (Harriet) just little.*

Ms. Ramirez: *So we can use what the mom does and says—or in this case, didn't say and didn't do—to help us understand what's in her heart (cognitive process focus).*

Clarisse: *That's not what my mom says!*

Ms. Ramirez: *That's a good point, Clarisse. Some of you had ideas pop into your heads that distracted you; they made you think about your own stories. Clarisse had to stop and ask herself how the ideas in her head could help her say something meaningful that would help us understand this story. Together with Jesse, she realized that this mom reacted differently than her mom. She used the idea that popped into her head—her spilling and her mom's reactions— to compare Harriet's mom's actions to her*

mom's, and then say something meaningful:
this mom is different (purposeful talk focus).
Then the rest of you used this to think about
what the mom says and does, and this gave
you an insight into what's in the mom's heart
(cognitive process focus). Hold on to this
thinking, and let's keep reading.

These second graders needed strong support to determine if the thoughts in their heads were helping with meaning making or distracting from the job. Even when the ideas that popped into some heads could help, students needed support in understanding how. This is not unusual for our younger learners. They simply need continued supportive opportunities to develop the ability to make these distinctions for themselves.

Likewise, the students' abilities to use what a character does, says, and thinks to understand what is in his or her heart is just developing. This means many more lessons designed to engage students with both focus points, first with heavy teacher and peer support and then eventually with lessening support, will be necessary.

Deconstructing the Lesson

- **How does the lesson design balance the focus on talk with the focus on cognitive processes?**

  As Sylvia orchestrated the conversation during this lesson, she asked the students to consider the meaningfulness of their ideas. She nudged the students to ignore distracting thoughts and helped them shape meaningful ideas. These ideas strengthened their thinking about the text to make inferences about the characters and then focus their talk. As the students talked about these initial realizations about the characters, their understanding grew stronger.

- **How does the teacher step in and out of the conversation to teach the use of purposeful talk without interrupting the construction of meaning?**

  Sylvia coached students to pause in their talking to reflect and determine whether they had constructed an idea that pushed the meaning-making forward. She stepped in to support the students before the talk was taken in the wrong direction during partnerships and whole-group talk, and then backed out when the talk was back on target. Her support was heavy in this lesson, particularly with respect to the talk focus.

- **How is responsibility for purposeful talk behaviors transferred to the students?**

The students are reminded of the role of their talk in constructing understanding and are asked to consider this during turn and talks. Sylvia monitored the turn and talk, coached students whose talk was moving in the wrong direction, and offered support right at the moment of need. As the students are in the beginning stages with this talk behavior, the need for this heavy level of support was anticipated and should lessen over time.

- **How are the students made aware of the link between cognitive processes, purposeful talk behavior, and the construction of meaning?**

The debrief at the end of this portion of the lesson helped students see clearly the way Clarisse used their talk focus—say something meaningful—to share just the part of her thinking that truly pushes the construction of meaning. Then Sylvia points out that by thinking through the lens of the cognitive process focus—using what characters do, say, and think (i.e., inferring)—the students together shaped Clarisse's idea into an understanding of the mom. Many more opportunities to think and talk in these ways, with the process made visible through debriefs, will continue to strengthen the students' awareness of the link between cognitive processes and talking in smart ways about their ideas.

Lesson 3

Purposeful Talk Behavior: Listening with Intent and Keeping Lines of Thinking Alive

When we have a powerful thought that we keenly want to share with others, our tendency is to focus fully on both the content of that thought and devise a means to express it—so fully that we often neglect to focus on other ideas being expressed. For students to progress to the point in their purposeful talk abilities where they are keeping lines of thinking alive, they first need to learn to actually listen to others' ideas. Often this means temporarily parking their own thoughts while they engage with someone else's. Truly listening to each other's ideas enables an element of purposefulness, or intent. We listen to others with the intent of understanding their ideas and developing stronger ideas from them. To do this, we must actively engage with the ideas— asking questions, adding on, pushing back, or simply asking for more information if we don't understand. Because we listen with the intent of understanding and working with an idea, teachers often pair listening with intent and keeping lines of thinking alive when teaching purposeful talk.

The teacher's role in this work includes checking in with students to be sure they are listening and helping them learn to monitor this for themselves. Once all have really listened to an idea, the teacher orchestrates the talk so it stays focused on that idea as students clarify, add onto, and push back at the thinking.

Classroom Context

A lively fourth-grade class was beginning a study of author's purpose and point of view and the choices authors make based on this. These students were eager talkers and had come a long way in ensuring that all participated in the talk and that the ideas they shared were meaningful.

Their classroom teacher, Don Reed, was masterful at selecting engaging texts, and it quickly became clear that the students had definite opinions about the topics and ideas in each text—so definite that they were focused only on sharing their own thoughts as opposed to listening to other perspectives. So not only were the students not listening to each other, but the popcorn-like throwing out of "I think" statements were about their own opinions, with no one working toward determining the author's purpose and point of view.

By the third lesson, Don and I realized that we needed to add a purposeful talk focus for listening with intent and sustaining effort around one student's idea to ensure that the students paused long enough to develop an understanding of that idea, and then shift the focus to whether the author seemed to be saying the same thing. This focus on the author's words, we hoped, would allow the author's purpose and point of view to emerge. Note that we in no way wanted the students to keep from developing their own beliefs on the topics or issues. Rather, we want the students to learn to read critically, distill what an author is saying and attempting to do with a text, and use this information wisely as they form their own opinions.

Interestingly enough, many of these students had focused on listening with intent and keeping lines of thinking alive in previous years. However, the class contained eight students new to the school, and several had personalities that enabled them to become the more dominant talkers in the room.

The text selected for this lesson was *Panther: Shadow of the Swamp* by Jonathan London (2000). This gorgeous narrative nonfiction picture book immerses the reader in the Florida Everglades, inviting him or her to tiptoe alongside a panther hunting for a meal. Don knew that some of his students would think panthers were decidedly cool, while others would immediately dislike them because panthers kill other animals.

On the following four pages you will see a lesson plan for Lesson 3. Following the lesson plan you will find the lesson narrative. Then you will come to a section titled Deconstructing the Lesson.

Lesson Plan—Teaching Purposeful Talk Behavior to Support the Construction of Meaning

Cognitive Process Focus: *(This is the way(s) of thinking and talking about reading that the students are learning in order to support the construction of meaning.)*

Understanding an author's purpose, point of view, and the choices he or she makes with a text help us better understand the text.

Text: *Panther: Shadow of the Swamp* by Jonathan London

Introduction: *(Include the cognitive process focus, the talk behavior that will be used to develop ideas, and text introduction.)*

We're studying the way readers determine what an author's point of view about his or her topic or issue might be, his or her purpose for writing, the decisions he or she makes based on this, and most importantly, how this affects us as readers. So far we've discovered that focusing on the author's word choices, facts he or she includes and doesn't include, and the photographs and illustrations helps us. I'm noticing that as we work to understand the author's point of view, some of you are letting your own opinions about the topic or issue override what the author is actually saying. As we think and talk today, we're going to revisit the need to truly listen to each

Stopping place	Cue for getting the talk started	Desired-response possibilities
cover (start the students anticipating)	What are you thinking? What are you expecting? What do you think the author means by "shadow of the swamp"? What does the illustration get you thinking or feeling? That's the illustrator's interpretation. Does it match yours?	This must be about panthers. The swamp must be where they live. Maybe the author is going to tell us all about both. The picture on the cover makes it all look beautiful. Maybe the author is going to talk about that, too.
page that ends with "but more than hunger drives her." (theorize about the author's purpose, point of view, and choices)	What are you thinking? Is this text different from some of the other nonfiction that we've read? Why do you think Jonathan London chose to write it this way? What was the author referring to with the words *shadow of the swamp*? "More than hunger drives her"—what does the author mean? What are you noticing about the author's words? The illustrations? Do you have any sense yet of how the author feels or wants us to feel?	Oh, the shadow is the panther. It's sneaking to hunt. This book is really different from the other nonfiction we've read. It has beautiful words—almost like poetry. And it's like a picture book, too. This makes the panther seem really awesome. "Drives her" means "keeps her going"—she is hunting for another reason. I wonder why. The author uses such beautiful and calm words. Maybe that's a hint about his purpose and point of view.
page that ends with "since early morning." (strengthen or change theory about the author's purpose, point of view, and choices)	What are you thinking? Why didn't the panther go after the armadillo? How do the author's words make you feel about the panther? Do you think this is the author's point of view, too? Why did the author write this?	The panther is really hungry, but she isn't hunting just anything. The author says the panther wants something big to eat now. I wonder why? She must be extra hungry. It makes me almost feel sorry for her. Maybe that's what the author wants. He wants us to care. Maybe that's why he wrote the book this way.

Purposeful Talk Focus: *(This is the talk behavior the students are focused on in support of the construction of meaning.)*
listening with intent and keeping lines of thinking alive

Goal: *(This is the meaning that students are thinking and talking toward.)*
Panthers are incredible creatures that need our protection (one of many possible big ideas).

Introduction *(cont.):* other and build on ideas. This means that when someone is speaking, you need to temporarily park your thinking on the side of your brain, and focus fully on that person so you really hear and think about his or her idea before we move on. As we build on his or her idea, we're going to compare his or her thinking to the author's so we begin to develop an understanding of what this author's purpose and point of view are. Then we'll move on to other ideas. The text we'll be reading, thinking, and talking about is *Panther: Shadow of the Swamp* by Jonathan London.

Anticipating talk difficulties	Support if necessary
• Students arguing for their own point of view vs. exploring ideas to uncover the author's purpose and point of view • Students sharing big cat facts— may need to remind them to say something meaningful	Model think-aloud: I'm looking at this drawing of the panther. I always thought they were fierce, but this animal looks calm, almost a little sad. That's what the illustrator thinks. And the title, *Shadow of the Swamp,* it sounds almost magical. Hmmm… this all gets me thinking that the author must have a specific point of view about panthers.
	Model think-aloud: This author talks about the panther and its home with such beautiful words. The language is very different from other nonfiction that we've read. This is written more like a picture book with beautiful illustrations. This makes me think about the panther in a very special way. I think that's why Jonathan London chose to write this type of text—a narrative nonfiction. Describing the panther as a shadow makes me think about what a skilled hunter it is. It sounds like such an incredible animal.
	Reread some phrases and model think-aloud about them, showing the way the words help you determine what the author thinks about the topic, and how the author uses words purposefully to shape your thoughts. Notice that the illustrations show how the illustrator interpreted the author's feelings.

(chart continues on the next page)

Lesson Plan (cont.)

Stopping place	Cue for getting the talk started	Desired-response possibilities
the end	What are you thinking? How are you feeling about the panther now? Has your thinking about the author's point of view changed, or were we on the right track? How did the author's words affect you? Does this have anything to do with the author's purpose?	That's why the author said it was more than hunger that makes her keep hunting. She has to care for her babies. Panthers are good moms. The panther looked mean when it killed the boar, but it was caring for its babies. The author wanted us to know that. He thinks they're really special, and he's getting us to care, too. I can tell because he only tells good things about them. That's on purpose.
after the factual information on the last page	What are you thinking? Why did the author include this information? Does this make his point of view stronger and support his purpose? Does it support our thinking about his purpose and point of view, or do we need to rethink our decisions?	These facts help me know that the author really does care about the panther. He wants us to know that they're in trouble, and he wants us to care, too. The story made us care, and the facts make us worry.

Process Debrief: (State the cognitive processes and talk behavior that enabled the construction of meaning.)

As we read, we worked to determine the author's point of view about panthers and why he might have written this book. We focused on his words, the facts he shared, and the things he didn't go deeply into, like killing the boar. The illustrator's interpretation helped us also; we should add that to our list of strategies on our chart for figuring out an author's purpose and point of view.

To think about these things together, we had to really listen and stay focused on one person's idea, think it through, and compare it to the text before we moved on to other ideas. Once we understood what someone was thinking and why, we compared that thinking with what the author seemed to be doing in the text. This helped us put aside our own points of view and focus on the author's words and information.

Anticipating talk difficulties	Support if necessary
	Focus on the page of the panther with her cubs. Reread and ask the students to think about the panther as a mother. Compare this to the panther killing the boar, and model think. Notice that although the picture looks scary, the author doesn't really describe the kill. Maybe the author didn't want us to focus on this. He wanted us to think more about the caring side of the panther.
	Model think-aloud: This information helps me know that Jonathan London is worried about both the Everglades and the panther. He really does think they deserve special care, and I think he's telling us so we will care for both, too. He is trying to persuade us.

Meaning Debrief: *(This is the meaning that students constructed.)*

We think this text is really about the author's belief that panthers are special animals that need protection. The author made choices that were very persuasive, and they worked on us. Now we're wondering how we can help (one of many possibilities).

Notes and Reflection: *(State observations that help with the design of future lessons, text selection, small-group support, and/or individual student support.)*

- Students need a high level of support with listening with intent. Some students who are listening well are beginning to make progress with keeping lines of thinking alive.
- Students are beginning to develop an awareness of clues that point to the author's purpose and point of view.

Lesson Narrative

Don paused after reading the words "but more than hunger drives her," a hint at the panther's motivation to hunt, to initiate talk. He barely got the "what" portion of "What are you thinking?" out of his mouth before Devin took over.

Devin: *I know about panthers. They're meat eaters, kinda like tigers. See, they run good, so they can catch stuff— prey…*

Mr. Reed: *Devin, can you use what you know to help us understand this text?*

Devin: *Well, it's what he said about the other animals— how they all disappear.*

Chantel: *Like what he said about the snakes and turtles?*

Devin: *Yeah! That's why he said it!*

Melinda: *Ohhh, that's mean! I think it's what the author thinks. He's telling us it (the panther) kills them (the prey).*

Devin: *No, because…it's…it's a meat eater. That's what they do. They gotta eat.*

Mr. Reed: *It sounds like you two each has your own point of view about panthers. But what does this author think? Let's go back to what Melinda said. She had a theory about the author's point of view. Did everyone really listen?*

All: *A mix of yeses, nos, and kindas.*

Mr. Reed: *You'd better ask Melinda to repeat her idea (purposeful talk focus). Don looked expectantly around the circle and waited for a student to take the incentive.*

Joseph: *What did you say?*

Melinda: *Well, um…it's…I said it's mean, and it's how the author thinks, because it's killing animals.*

Mr. Reed: *So is there any evidence so far that the author thinks panthers are mean? (Devin slowly and with great* exaggeration shakes head no.) *That this is the author's point of view, too? (cognitive process focus) Turn and talk to your partner.*

Don listens in to partners as they talk, supporting a few by rereading a portion of the text to them, and then asks Trevian to begin the whole-group talk.

Trevian: *Me and my partner, we don't think so because it's just facts. The author didn't make it scary or anything to sound mean. He just says the other animals get out of the way when it (the panther) comes. He just tells facts.*

Mr. Reed: *Trevian is disagreeing with Melinda. What do the rest of you think?*

Alex: *If he wanted us to think it was mean, he would say the facts different, like…*

Mia: *Yeah, like with mean words.*

Anna: *And he said it's hungry. That's not mean—to be hungry.*

Mr. Reed: *So this is Melinda's point of view, but it sounds like you don't think there's any evidence to lead us to believe it's also the author's point of view. Mia, you brought up a good point. You said the author didn't tell about the panther in a mean way. We know we can use word choice as a clue to help us figure out point of view. How do the author's words help?*

Don rereads the last two pages so the students are able to contemplate the author's word choice. Through conversation, they come to the conclusion that the words are lyrical and calming—what the students call smooth instead of scary—but they also make the panther sound strong. Don then comes back to Melinda to see if the conversation had any effect on her.

Mr. Reed: *Melinda, what do you think?*

Melinda: *Yeah, but I still kinda think it's mean.*

Charlie: *But you're supposed to think about how the author thinks, not you!*

Melinda: *Oh yeah…*

Don: *Ah! Because we slowed down and really listened, we were able to think about Melinda's idea, hold it up against the text, and find that while this is what Melinda thinks, it didn't seem to be the author's point of view. We formed the new idea that came from the talking and now we have a firmer theory about the author's point of view. Hold onto this as we keep reading, and listen for evidence to support or disprove our theory. We'll check with Melinda, too, to see if her point of view changes.*

By the end of the read-aloud, the students concluded that the author felt the panther is an amazing and caring animal that deserves our respect. It seemed that through the inclusion of specific facts and careful word choice, he was trying to persuade us to feel the same way. Melinda even conceded that panthers aren't that mean if they're hunting to care for their babies.

As in the previous two lessons, the students will need many more highly supported learning experiences with the purposeful talk focus to fall back into the habit (or learn the habit, for the new students) of listening with intent and developing ideas.

Deconstructing the Lesson

- **How does the lesson design balance the focus on talk with the focus on cognitive processes?**

  The students highlighted in this lesson needed to rethink their need to listen with intent and keep lines of thinking alive in order to use talk more purposefully. This slowed them down enough to begin taking on the cognitive process focus—determining author's purpose, point of view, and the decisions authors make based on this. In this case, the talk focus supported the cognitive process focus.

- **How does the teacher step in and out of the conversation to teach the use of purposeful talk without interrupting the construction of meaning?**

  As anticipated, the first comments were a mix of facts and

personal points of view. Don asked Devin to use what he knew to say something meaningful. This allowed Devin's thoughts to become the impetus for delving deeper into the author's thinking. His idea prompted Melinda's theory about the author's point of view. Don took control of the conversation, asking students to pause and listen to her idea (knowing that they hadn't listened the first time), and then partner-talk. The first students to talk with the whole group disagreed with Melinda's reasoning and presented a second theory about the author's point of view. Don asked the students to keep this line of thinking alive, then stepped back and allowed the talk to flow before redirecting again. Note that if the students had not been able to stay focused on the idea, he would have stepped back in, asking them to add on to develop it even more.

- **How is responsibility for purposeful talk behaviors transferred to the students?**

Don set the expectation that the students would take responsibility for the purposeful talk focus by having them ask Melinda to repeat her idea so they could listen with intent. Doing this was not only necessary for taking on the cognitive process focus and constructing meaning, but it's an important step in building the habit of listening with intent. The teacher checked several other times during the lesson to be sure the students had listened and had them ask for the idea to be repeated if they had not. While this does slow down the pace of the lesson, it eventually enables stronger work as the habit of listening improves.

- **How are students made aware of the link between cognitive processes, purposeful talk behavior, and the construction of meaning?**

The quick debrief before delving back into the text helped the students understand the importance of listening, sticking with an idea, and developing it. These quick debriefs at the end of each pause to think and talk together, along with a more detailed debrief at the end of the lesson, play a vital role in making explicit for students what they have accomplished and how.

Lesson 4

Purposeful Talk Behavior: Negotiating Meaning

As students develop their abilities to keep lines of thinking alive, we up the intensity of the talk and the depth of understanding that the students construct. We coach them to think and talk through an idea to its fullest potential. This requires the students to dig deeper into the reasons for their thinking and weigh their thinking against the thoughts of others.

As when students are focusing on keeping lines of thinking alive, this process includes asking them to substantiate their ideas with evidence from the text alone or a mix of the text and other sources. We nudge others to question if more information is needed for clarity or more evidence is needed to substantiate the idea, and weigh in with agreement or disagreement. However, agreeing or disagreeing without adding to the accumulating understanding is not enough. Those who agree are encouraged to articulate their reasoning and add supporting evidence to the conversation. We balance this with those who disagree, requiring the same reflection and evidence to push away from the idea.

As a variety of voices weigh in, we strengthen the idea as much as possible if all are in agreement and wonder if there might be other voices elsewhere who would disagree with us. Or we begin to think and talk about our own differing viewpoints, working to see if we are able to come to a consensus. This requires a willingness to be flexible and thoughtfully consider others' points of view. (Note the importance of listening with intent in this process.) It's important to realize that consensus is not always possible or necessary. As with adults in the world outside of school, students will form different beliefs and at times must agree to disagree. What's most important is not agreement, but learning to develop a logical, well-thought-out position based on evidence and rich, lively discussion.

Negotiating meaning takes time, so we need to be particular about the points in a conversation where we push toward this depth of effort and understanding. In general, we nudge the students into negotiation as the conversation approaches critical understandings that build toward deeper meanings in the text and of our world.

Classroom Context

For this lesson, we join a fifth-grade class in mid-spring as they study the genre of biography. To construct a deep understanding of the subject of a biography, the students are learning to draw together a variety of cognitive processes that enable deep understanding of both fiction and nonfiction texts. This includes inferences that help us understand the interplay among setting, events, and characters and their motives, as well as detecting an author's purpose and point of view and determining the central ideas, and then focus on synthesizing all of this information to develop our own points of view about the individual.

Listening to her students thinking and talking about biographies for two weeks led their teacher, Cheryl McMann, to the realization that the students were treading on the surface of understanding the people they were reading, thinking, and talking about. She knew she needed to support the students in taking their ideas to greater depth. This lesson would be the students' first exposure to a deeper negotiation of meaning.

The biography *Stealing Home: Jackie Robinson: Against the Odds* by Robert Burleigh (2007) was chosen for this lesson. This nontraditional biography is actually a mixed-genre text in which the author imparts a sense of the man with a lyrical narrative that describes Robinson's legendary base stealing, supplemented by separate biographical insets on each page. Planning to read this text aloud required extra thought. What should be read first, the narrative or biographical information? All the biographical information or selected insets? For this particular group of students, we chose to begin with the narrative, use it to gain some sense of Robinson and the author's purpose and point of view, and then move into some of the biographical information, with a continuation the next day.

On the following four pages you will see a lesson plan for Lesson 4. Following the lesson plan you will find the lesson narrative. Then you will come to a section titled Deconstructing the Lesson.

Lesson Plan—Teaching Purposeful Talk Behavior to Support the Construction of Meaning

Cognitive Process Focus: *(This is the way(s) of thinking and talking about reading that the students are learning in order to support the construction of meaning.)*

Inferring and synthesizing to understand the author's point of view, and developing our own point of view about the subject of a biography

Text: *Stealing Home: Jackie Robinson: Against the Odds* by Robert Burleigh

Introduction: *(Include the cognitive process focus, the talk behavior that will be used to develop ideas, and text introduction.)*

We're going to continue our study of the ways we think and talk in order to understand the subject of a biography. We know that we need to consider the interplay among setting, characters, and events to understand what affects and motivates the person we are learning about. We also need to determine the author's purpose and point of view so we are able to judge the information and use it smartly.

You've been working very hard to really listen to each other and think and talk about each other's ideas. Today we're going to begin a biography about Jackie Robinson. As our thinking and talking helps us understand Jackie Robinson, we're going to dig a little deeper into our ideas. I'm going to ask you to really consider whether you agree with the idea or ideas being discussed and why. We need to learn to be aware of what is making us think a certain way, decide if other ideas are a possibility, build the ideas as strong as possible, and then push back and forth if we don't agree. Your job will always be to listen, consider what is being said, and be willing to think about other points of view. This will help you make up your own mind and understand exactly why you feel a certain way.

Stopping place	Cue for getting the talk started	Desired-response possibilities
after reading the narrative in its entirety (to build a beginning sense of who Jackie Robinson is and the author's purpose and point of view)	What are you thinking? What does this author seem to think about Jackie Robinson? What does the author mean at the end—baseball and America will never be the same?	Jackie is stealing bases; that's hard to do! The author makes it sound so exciting—with all the people cheering for Jackie and the way he described Jackie running. The author makes him seem amazing. I think that's his point of view, and maybe he tells it in such an exciting way so we'll think so, too. The author also said baseball and America will never be the same. Something changed them—but I don't know what yet.
Then and Now (construct stronger theories about Robinson and understand the way of the world at the time)	What are you thinking? What is the author telling us about the world back then? What does this have to do with Jackie Robinson?	Things were different back then. Black people and white people didn't get along. The author said black people couldn't play baseball. That's not fair. But Jackie Robinson did play baseball. How? The author said something about change. Maybe Jackie is a person who changed things.
Jack of All Sports (construct stronger theories about Robinson)	What are you thinking? How does this go with our thinking after reading the narrative text? How did the ways of the world back then affect Jackie?	Wow, he was a great athlete. The part of the text that was all about base stealing, along with this information, is helping me understand how good he was. Today he could play on a lot of teams and make a lot of money. But back then he couldn't. That must have made him really mad! I wonder how he handled it.

Purposeful Talk Focus: *(This is the talk behavior the students are focused on in support of the construction of meaning.)*
Listening with intent and keeping lines of thinking alive

Goal: *(This is the meaning that students are thinking and talking toward.)*
Courage and strong beliefs can change the world for the better (one of many possible themes or big ideas).

Introduction *(cont.)*: Our biography of Jackie Robinson, called *Stealing Home: Jackie Robinson: Against the Odds* by Robert Burleigh, is an unusual one. It's a mixed-genre text (show students while explaining) with narrative at the top of the page and bits of biographical information below. I'm going to read the narrative first. We'll think and talk about it together, and then move into some of the biographical information, merging our ideas from the biographical text with our thinking from the narrative text. It will take us two days to read, think, and talk through the whole text.

Anticipating talk difficulties	Support if necessary
• Students sharing factual information without using it to build toward the construction of meaning • Students clinging to their own opinions without a willingness to entertain a different perspective • Students becoming overly argumentative	Model think-aloud: I'm noticing that the author writes in a way that makes me feel the action and excitement of Jackie's base stealing. The writing feels fast—like Jackie Robinson. I feel like the author is really excited about this person and might be writing in a way that will make me excited, too. Reread—listen to the last page again. This tells me that something happens that changes a lot of things. I wonder what.
	Reread—"Baseball of course was only a bite-sized picture of mid-twentieth century American life." Hmmm... I think the author is telling me something about the world back then. This was 1946, and I know this was before the civil rights era. Black and white people didn't get along. But the last two lines make me think Jackie is going to change this.
	Model think-aloud: Great athletes today have so many opportunities to play. I wonder how it would feel to be great and not get a chance because of the color of your skin. What do you think? How would this make Jackie feel? *(chart continues on the next page)*

Lesson Plan *(cont.)*

Stopping place	Cue for getting the talk started	Desired-response possibilities
"Dem Bums" Ain't Bums No More (construct stronger theories about Robinson and his motives)	What are you thinking? Why do you think the Brooklyn Dodgers let Jackie play?	Oh, now I'm getting this. Jackie was so good that the Dodgers needed him. They let him play even though he was black so they could win. He really wanted to play. I wonder if Jackie liked it?
Dodgers vs. Yankees: Classic Battles! (construct stronger theories about Robinson and his motives)	What are you thinking? How do you think people felt about Jackie?	Oh, this must be what the part of the text about change was talking about. It sounds like Jackie was becoming famous. Today everybody would love him. I wonder if that's true because of the way of the world back then.
"I'm Looking for a Ballplayer with Guts Enough Not To Fight Back!" (construct stronger theories about Robinson and his motives and the motives of others)	What are you thinking? What did the manager mean by "guts enough not to fight back"? Why would Jackie say yes? What does this tell us about him?	The manager wanted someone who wouldn't fight back because the white people didn't want black people to play. Jackie said yes because he wanted to change things. He wanted black athletes to get a chance. And it worked; the book said other black players got a chance to play after Jackie said yes. That means he's brave and probably has a lot of self-control. Maybe we can be like him.

Process Debrief: *(State the cognitive processes and talk behavior that enabled the construction of meaning.)*

Today we took time to better understand Jackie, from both the author's point of view and our own, build our ideas stronger, and think about different points of view. To do this, we listened to each other, asked questions, and searched for evidence. We're finding out that there are different possible interpretations of the same information, and tomorrow we'll continue to see if both or all can be supported and develop our own points of view. When we take the time to listen to the thinking behind different ideas, our own thinking grows stronger and may even change over time.

Anticipating talk difficulties	Support if necessary
	Model think-aloud: As I read this, I'm wondering if the Dodgers just let Jackie play because he was such a great athlete and they needed him to win. I think this is what the author meant about baseball changing, but I'm wondering about why it changed. I wonder how Jackie felt about this.
	Model think-aloud: So it sounds like Jackie made a huge difference to the team. I wonder if people loved him because he helped them win even though he was black, or if they still didn't want him to play. I know fans love it when their team is winning, but…
	Model think-aloud: "I'm looking for a ballplayer with guts enough not to fight back!" I know *guts* mean "courage." Why would the manager not want Jackie to fight back, and why would he need courage to do this? Maybe thinking about the way of the world back then will help us.

Meaning Debrief: *(This is the meaning that students constructed.)*

So far, we think this text is really about the power of courage and believing in ourselves. We're understanding that Jackie Robinson was a very brave man, for many reasons. We're beginning to wonder what we can learn from him. We'll read more tomorrow and think more about this (one of many possibilities).

Notes and Reflection: *(State observations that help with the design of future lessons, text selection, small-group support, and/or individual student support.)*

- The lesson ran long due to the amount of talk. Consider planning a series of lessons over several days using the next text.
- The students need heavy teacher support with negotiating meaning. I will need to continue this focus over many more lessons.

Lesson Narrative

We join the conversation as Cheryl and the students finish reading the section titled "I'm Looking for a Ballplayer with Guts Enough Not To Fight Back!" This bit of biographical information holds some critical insight into not only the circumstances that brought Jackie Robinson to the Brooklyn Dodgers, but his calm restraint in trying situations. At this point, the students had constructed theories about the author's point of view as well as the way that people's beliefs, the cultures of the time, and specific events affected Robinson.

Joshua: *He said he'll need guts—that's saying courage—because white people won't like that he's getting to play.*

Ms. McMann: *So why do you think Jackie agreed? What does this tell us about him (cognitive process focus)?*

Joshua: *He said yes so he can play.*

Jonathan: *No, no, I think…*

Ms. McMann: *Ah, Jonathan, it sounds like you have a different idea?*

Jonathan: *(shakes head yes)*

Ms. McMann: *Will you hold onto it until we dig into Joshua's idea? Let's hear his evidence before we move on to a new idea. Joshua, what makes you think that's the reason?*

Joshua: *Because he was the star in college—but he couldn't be on a team because of racism.*

Ms. McMann: *What do the rest of you think?*

Kayla: *It said that was how the world was back then. So he had to say yes, because he could get a chance (to play). He couldn't get a chance before. They didn't care he was the star because he was black.*

Jonathan: *But Kayla, he… well, he… yeah, he probably*

	did want to play, but it's like Martin Luther King Jr. He always said don't fight. And the book said…
Theresea:	*Oh! It's like* The Other Side *(referring to the book by Jacqueline Woodson, which the students had read, thought, and talked about together)! It said about the wall—on the other page (referring to the "Then and Now" section). It's like the fence. He (Jackie Robinson) knows it shouldn't be.*
Marta:	*Oh, yeah. I didn't think about that!*
Ms. McMann:	*So you're constructing a new theory for why Jackie agreed not to fight back (cognitive process focus). What does everyone think about this idea (looking questioningly around the circle)?*
Ben:	*No, I don't get it—what Theresea said.*
Ms. McMann:	*When you don't understand what someone said, remember, it's your job to ask them to explain.*
Ben:	*(looking at Theresea) I don't get what you mean.*
Theresea:	*Like in that book (The Other Side), the girls sat on the fence and the fence was supposed to be like racism. But the fence didn't work… it…they climbed up on it and over it, and they played anyway.*
Ms. McMann:	*So, how is that like Jackie?*
Rosie:	*I get what you mean! It's like Jackie played with them (the Brooklyn Dodgers) to show there shouldn't be racism.*
Theresea:	*Yeah, that's why he said yes.*
Jonathan:	*That's like what I think.*
Ms. McMann:	*So, you're agreeing? Can you add to our thinking (purposeful talk focus)?*

Jonathan:	*Well, it's better to show how to do it than just tell it.*
Cheryl:	*So, we have two different points of view. We're thinking Jackie may have agreed not to fight back so he could play baseball on a professional team, or maybe he said yes to prove racism is wrong. What do the rest of you think (purposeful talk focus)?*

A buzz breaks out in the room as the students consider the two possibilities. Hearing the noise level escalate with excitement, Cheryl asks the students to turn and talk with their partners. When they regroup, the students have thoughts to support both points of view. With Cheryl's support, they push and pull at the ideas, offering evidence from *Stealing Home*, *The Other Side*, and what they know to be true of that era and the world today. It became clear that there was ample evidence to support both views, with some students leaning more toward one or the other and many in between, not yet able to definitively say that Jackie's decision was based on one reason or the other. Cheryl decided to steer the conversation toward the second of her original questions.

Ms. McMann:	*Well, if Jackie agreed not to fight back just so he would have an opportunity to play, what does this tell us about him? (cognitive process focus)*
Joshua:	*He's a winner. He wants to play and win. No matter what—he's just gotta play.*
Ben:	*That's like baseball now—and football and stuff, too. They always want to just win.*
Ms. McMann:	*What if he said yes to prove a point about racism? What would that tell us about him?*
Tanya:	*That's what we're saying. He's like Martin Luther King Jr. He wants peace between blacks and whites, and he's going to prove how.*
Devon:	*Yeah, he's like a peacemaker. He doesn't fight.*

Ms. McMann:	*I'm wondering if both of these may be possibilities. Could Jackie be a winner— someone who wants to play no matter what— and a peacemaker who shows others by setting a good example?*
Devon:	*Well, but he didn't give speeches and stuff. That's what Martin Luther King Jr. did.*
Tanya:	*But he could still care even if he didn't give a speech. And he might. We didn't finish (reading the book) yet. He could care about playing and want to be peace…I mean, want to get peace.*
Ms. McMann:	*Should we hold onto both theories about Jackie for now, and we'll keep reading and thinking about this tomorrow?*
Tanya:	*Yeah, I guess. He could be both, but I still think he just wants peace.*

This willingness to hold onto both possibilities, while not overwhelming, is a first step in developing the flexibility needed to consider alternative points of view when evidence merits it. As they read, thought, and talked together the next day, the students came to believe that both theories about Jackie's motive for agreeing not to fight back could indeed be true. Again they used evidence from Burleigh's *Stealing Home* (2007), Jacqueline Woodson's *The Other Side* (2001), and their understanding of the world during this era and of the world today.

Deconstructing the Lesson

- **How does the lesson design balance the focus on talk with the focus on cognitive processes?**

  As the students worked to understand Jackie's motives for agreeing not to fight, a difference of opinions arose. Understanding Jackie's motive is a critical step in understanding him, so this was the perfect place to nudge students into a negotiation of meaning. Through the consideration of both ideas, the students developed a greater understanding of the person and the power of purposeful talk.

- **How does the teacher step in and out of the conversation to teach the use of purposeful talk without interrupting the construction of meaning?**

In this snippet of the talk, Cheryl became the holder of the two ideas being constructed. She reminded the students of the two possible theories, restating them so the students were able to clearly think and talk about them. As the students grow accustomed to this, the responsibility for holding onto multiple ideas will be transferred to them, but for now, their efforts are focused on thinking flexibly between the two.

- **How is responsibility for purposeful talk behaviors transferred to the students?**

At the beginning of the conversation, Jonathan wanted to suggest an alternative to Joshua's idea before the idea had a chance to build. Cheryl politely but directly asked Jonathan to hold his thinking for a moment while Joshua offered evidence to complete his idea, reminding Jonathan of the need to keep a line of thinking alive. Later in the conversation, the students were not truly listening to one another. The teacher reminded one student of his role and had him take responsibility for having the information repeated. These little reminders help students build the habits necessary to independently engage in purposeful talk independently.

- **How are the students made aware of the link between cognitive processes, purposeful talk behavior, and the construction of meaning?**

Through talk, the students learn that although they were all inferring from and synthesizing the same factual information, that information may be interpreted in different ways by different individuals. What will become more and more obvious to the students over time is that listening to each idea, allowing it to build to its fullest, and thinking about each, even if you don't initially agree, will allow your own thinking to change and strengthen.

Chapter 3

Creating Habits of Mind: Lessons That Teach Students to Read, Think, and Talk Independently

As students grow stronger in thinking and talking purposefully about their ideas, lessons should be designed to teach independence by gradually releasing responsibility—for both the cognitive processes they are learning and the behaviors that enable them to talk about their thinking and construct meaning.

As discussed in Chapter 1, this shift toward independence is crucial. The ability to think and talk with others to build and strengthen understanding is a social process that will enable success in a wide range of contexts beyond the classroom. Learning to participate in and orchestrate purposeful conversations on their own will encourage students to access a wide range of input as they work toward and hover at the edge of important understandings and decisions throughout their lives. And in those instances when students do need to truly construct meaning independently, learning to use the echoes of past conversations will serve to guide the process.

How much independence students develop over the course of a year will depend greatly on the length of time they have been thinking and talking purposefully with others, as well as the precision of instruction designed to move their efforts toward that independence. Thinking about the amount of teacher support offered during the read-alouds in Chapter 2 helps us begin to outline the range of talk behaviors that students should gradually take control over. During the read-aloud, we support students by selecting the text, determining where to stop and talk, and cueing the students as to what they should be thinking and talking about and how. We also support them in using specific behaviors to talk purposefully, bundling up the talk, and deciding when meaning is strong enough to move on to the next step. Students need to learn not only how to make these decisions on their own, but also how to monitor their conversations and levels of understanding; this will help them to determine whether they are making smart decisions and truly constructing strong meaning. Moving students from a highly supported read-aloud to independent practice without gentle yet deliberate steps in between certainly will not enable success.

Creating Independence Using the Gradual Release of Responsibility Model

The gradual release of responsibility model (Pearson and Gallagher 1983) offers a framework for the thoughtful, measured turnover to the learner of greater amounts of responsibility for aspects of the ongoing work. This framework is comprised of instructional approaches and structures that gradually lessen the support of a proficient other (in this case, the teacher) as the learner develops awareness, knowledge, and strategic abilities with specific ways of thinking—and specific ways of talking about that thinking.

The read-aloud lessons featured in Chapter 2 allow for the highest level of support on this continuum. In addition to these lessons, we want our students reading, thinking, and talking with varying amounts of support throughout the reading workshop. Students should practice these ways of thinking and talking with increasing amounts of independence.

What follows is a series of instructional opportunities designed to gradually release responsibility for thinking and talking to the students, allowing them to take steps toward independence. To illustrate this gradual release over time, we'll continue to follow the fourth-grade class highlighted in Chapter 2. We left the lively group and their teacher, Don Reed, at the end of a read-aloud of

Panther: Shadow of the Swamp by Jonathan London. A cognitive process focus on author's purpose and point of view had been established, including the choices the author makes based on these, and a purposeful talk focus was established on listening with intent in order to keep a line of thinking alive.

The progression of lessons and vignettes that follow offers a glimpse of the group as they gradually take control of the thinking and talking through immersion in shared reading, guided reading, partner reading, and independent reading. While the class that was used to illustrate this progression along the release of responsibility continuum happens to be fourth grade, the process is representational of lesson design that supports students in taking control of the thinking and talking at any grade level. The text choices, cognitive process focuses, configuration of partnership opportunities, and the expectation for the amount of independence may vary by grade level, but also the mix of instructional approaches, thoughtful lesson design for each, and the importance of informative feedback remain constant. This continuous emphasis on both cognitive processes and purposeful talk behaviors not only supports students, but reminds us that we must be diligent in nurturing the behaviors we hope will become habits.

Informative Feedback

A key to supporting students in developing independent abilities is informative feedback. Students learn to take charge, making decisions about text choice, how to think and talk their way through the texts, and how to judge their levels of meaning making. Giving feedback allows them to reflect on their use of the cognitive process focuses, talk behavior, and other strategies for navigating their way through a text.

In *Enriching Feedback in the Primary Classroom*, author Shirley Clarke reminds us, "We need to give specific feedback focusing on successes and improvement, rather than correction" (2003, 54). Sue Brown, author of *Shared Reading for Grades 3 and Beyond: Working It Out Together*, submits that "feedback should aim to increase the students' control of their own learning"

(2004, 87). In other words, effective feedback not only helps students see their successes and their next steps but it also helps them strategize their way through those steps. It is clear, explicit, and supportive and is always offered with the understanding that these are positive steps that will strengthen the learner.

Clarke agrees, offering, "Our aim is, of course, to involve students as far as possible in the analysis and constructive criticism of their own work. We want them to use self-evaluation continually, so that reflection, pride in successes, modification, and improvement become a natural part of the process of learning" (2003, 131). Simply said, we want our students to develop the ability to think and use talk purposefully on their own, as well as possess the reflective skills necessary to continue to strengthen their own abilities to do so.

During shared and guided reading, teacher feedback is offered in meaningful spurts throughout the lesson and then reiterated during the lesson debrief. As students work in partners with increased independence, they also need feedback aimed precisely at the edge of their current abilities. Reading conferences offer the ideal opportunity to effectively assess students' use of the cognitive processes and talk behaviors, and they offer the most specific feedback. Listening in on partner talk, nudging, and debriefing allows the teacher to assess, support if necessary, and offer feedback that keeps the partnership progressing in its ability to think and talk together. Engaging in conversations with students about reading and thinking as they read independently offers the clearest assessment of the degree of independence that each student has reached with his or her thinking (using the cognitive process focuses and echoes of past conversations). These conversations also offer crucial opportunities for the most precise feedback that will propel that student toward greater success.

Shared Reading

The first step along the release of responsibility continuum from the heavily supported read-aloud toward independence is *shared reading*. Shared reading can be used to release responsibility for many aspects of reading, such as developing independence with the reading process in beginning readers. Our focus here will be on helping students take control of thinking and talking their way through a text, both with a partner and eventually on their own.

During a read-aloud, the teacher supports the students' efforts to think and talk together through text selection, planning the progression through the text, questioning, orchestrating the talk, and modeling when necessary. Shared reading allows students the opportunity to develop an awareness of the decisions the teacher has been making on their behalf and gradually begin to shoulder some of the responsibility themselves. This work will include teaching students to make decisions about where to stop and talk with their partners (or stop, think, and prepare for partner talk) and why. It also involves teaching students to remember to think and talk through the lens of the cognitive process focuses, using specific talk behavior to talk purposefully about their thinking, organizing their own talk before progressing, and monitoring their own comprehension as they work to understand the text and use the text to understand their world.

As we involve students in the decisions that steer the thinking and talking, we also invite them into critical reflections on the process. This gives students the metacognitive insights that will strengthen their own decision making, their abilities to judge the depth of their own construction of meaning, and their understanding of the value of talking purposefully with others about their thinking.

During shared instructional opportunities, our role shifts from proficient model and orchestrator to side-by-side partner in the work. However, this shift is not absolute. The amount of support we offer during any instruction along the release of responsibility continuum will vary as students experience struggles and successes. If students are struggling, what we do not want to do is simplify the work. Rather, we step in with slight increases of support until the students are able to regain control. Likewise, if the students are capable of more independence than we had anticipated, we step back, turning more of the control over to them.

A possible first step for shared instruction is designing lessons that offer insights as to how readers plan their approaches to thinking and talking through a text. We often start our reading partnership with a scaffold for planning when to pause and talk about our thinking, such as stopping at the end of each page. Our goal is to teach students to recognize crucial information or developments in texts that merit conversation. Guide students through this process, along with letting the resulting ideas guide decisions about when to pause, think deeply, and talk. This will ensure that students will self-monitor and use purposeful talk to discuss aspects of the text that are vital for the construction of meaning.

In addition to gradually taking over responsibility for the planning of their reading, thinking, and talking using a range of cognitive processes, students will need to learn to be mindful of their own talk behavior. This includes orchestrating conversations to be sure that all voices are heard, their ideas actually contribute to the conversation, and lines of thinking are kept alive. Also, they must work to construct the strongest meaning possible.

As we rejoin Don and his fourth graders, we find them eight lessons into their focus on using purposeful talk, specifically listening with intent and keeping lines of thinking alive. This supports their efforts in determining author's purpose, point of view, and the decisions an author makes based on these. While the students were finding success in the heavily supported read-aloud, Don and I were not yet hearing evidence of the same strong thinking using the cognitive process focus in their partner talk or in their thinking and talking about their independent reading. And although the students were listening to each other, they were not lingering over ideas and allowing them to develop to their fullest potential. We felt it was time to initiate supportive instructional steps so that students could take responsibility for both the cognitive process focus and the specific talk behavior.

We began with shared instruction and chose a piece of text that was slightly easier than the text we had been using for read-alouds. Like most fourth-grade classrooms, this one includes a range of reading levels and English language learners. The release of responsibility was going to require students to access the text partially on their own, and we wanted all students to experience a degree of success. To ensure full participation in the thinking and talking, Don opted to display the text using the document camera and chose to read it aloud while the students followed with their eyes and in their heads. Other options for reading the text would have included having the students read silently for themselves, either from the document camera, an overhead projector, their own copies, or having partners read together.

The piece that was chosen, *The Coral Reef Crisis*, comes from Teacher Created Materials' *Write Time For Kids* (2000). This is a one-page piece of expository text cleanly laid out in three columns with clear headings differentiated from the running text with colored ink and vibrant photographs. The piece outlines the impending danger coral reefs are facing due to human behaviors, such as pollution, destructive fishing practices, and warming waters. The author's point of view is clear, and her purpose—a mix of informing and persuading—is one the students would be able to discern using strategies learned during the read-alouds.

As the students were in need of support with taking responsibility for both the cognitive process focus and their purposeful talk, we designed the lesson to move the students' thinking and talking from partnerships to whole-group conversation. Although moving from partner talk to whole-group talk throughout the lesson slows the pace down, listening to other partnerships share their processes and end results provides immediate feedback. This sharpens all learners' behavior on the very next think-and-talk opportunity. This continual shaping of the decisions around thinking and talking is what helps build the habits that eventually enable strong independent abilities. As an added bonus, moving from partnership talk to whole-group talk would also give us an opportunity to assess the partnerships. Gauging partnerships to ascertain which are working well, need additional support, or just need rethinking altogether is a continual process.

On the following four pages you will see a lesson plan demonstrating the release of responsibility model for thinking and talking about text. Following the lesson plan you will find the lesson narrative. A blank copy of the lesson plan is included in Appendix B for classroom use.

Lesson Plan—Release of Responsibility for Thinking and Talking About Texts

Cognitive Process Focus: *(This is the way(s) of thinking and talking about reading that the students are learning in order to support the construction of meaning.)*

Understanding an author's purpose and point of view and the choices he or she makes to support these helps us better understand the text.

Text: *The Coral Reef Crisis* by Ritu Upadhyay (Write Time For Kids, Level 3)

Supports: *(What aspects of this text will help students make meaning?)*

photographs, statement following the title, headings, strong word choice

Introduction: *(What will I say to set up the reading through the lens of our focus and meaning making?)*

Today you're going to begin taking more responsibility for determining the author's purpose, point of view, and the choices the author makes based on both of these, and using all of this to make stronger meaning. This is the same work we've been doing in read-alouds. But now, you and your partner will be making decisions about how to read the text, what to think and talk about to help you determine the author's purpose and point of view, and how to use this information to help you construct strong meaning. We'll all read portions

Stopping place	Cue for getting the talk started	Desired-response possibilities
Planning before we read	How should we go about reading, thinking, and talking about this piece?	My partner and I know we should always start with the title. And we think the photos show what we're going to read about; we want to look at those and think about them first. Then the author also has headings. Nonfiction authors give us headings to organize ideas, so we should read each heading and the section under it, then think more and talk about how it all goes together.
Thinking and talking through the reading: title, photos, and captions	What are you thinking? How do the title, photographs, and captions work together to get you thinking about ideas? Do they give you any clues about ideas in the text, the author's purpose, or the author's point of view?	We can tell we're going to read about the coral reef from the title and the photographs. We noticed the title has a scary word—*crisis.* A crisis is bad. But the large photograph is beautiful. It doesn't look like a crisis. At first we thought the little photographs were beautiful, too, but when we read the captions, we knew the author was showing us something bad. Maybe they have to do with the crisis. The big picture might be there so we know how beautiful the coral reef is and to make us care about the crisis. Maybe that's the author's purpose—to tell us that and make us care.
First section	What are you thinking? What's important to think and talk about in this section? Does this build on our thinking after we discussed the title and photographs?	My partner and I both thought the first paragraph made the coral reef sound incredible. The author used all words that sounded good. This part went with the large photograph. We think the author did that on purpose to make us love the coral reefs. And, he used the photograph on purpose to make us really care. But then, the second paragraph changed everything. It's all about danger and destroying and sea animals dying. The text says reefs are dying because of people and what they do. The author chose words that scare us to make us worried. He is trying to make us care. We thought that was persuading.

Purposeful Talk Focus: *(This is the talk behavior that the students are focused on in support of the construction of meaning.)*
listening with intent and developing ideas

Goal: *(This is the meaning that students are thinking and talking toward.)*
Because human behavior can inadvertently have a negative effect on our environment, people should take steps to protect special habitats.

Challenges: *(What aspects of this text might interfere with meaning making?)*
unfamiliarity with habitat

Introduction *(cont.)*: of the text together, then you and your partner will have time to think and talk. After you've had time to think and talk, we'll all come back together to discuss the meaning and what partners talked about to help them construct meaning. Remember, when you talk with your partner, you're going to need to be sure that both of you are sharing ideas that help you understand, and that you listen with intent and take the time to develop those ideas. This way, you and your partner will practice making decisions and using those decisions to guide your thinking and talking together. This will help you and your partner work together without me. It will also help you read and think smartly on your own.

Releasing responsibility: Process debrief and reflection possibilities

Look for opportunities to highlight partners who scanned the text, planned how they should read and talk using the features and the organization of the text, and made any other decisions about what to discuss that enabled strong meaning making.

Look for opportunities to highlight partners who listened with intent, formed ideas, and exhibited other purposeful talk behaviors.

Clearly link decisions and talk behavior to meaning making.

Look for opportunities to highlight partners who used the title, photos, heading, and captions to get a sense of what they would be reading; formed a theory about the author's point of view and the ideas that will be in the text; and made any other decisions about what to discuss that enabled strong meaning making.

Look for opportunities to highlight partners who listened with intent, formed ideas, and exhibited other purposeful talk behaviors.

Clearly link decisions and talk behavior to meaning making.

Look for opportunity to highlight partners who talked about new ideas and how these ideas built on or made them rethink their theories, noticed strong word choice, talked about what the author was doing; note any other decisions about what to discuss that enabled strong meaning making.

Look for opportunity to highlight partners who listened with intent, formed ideas, and exhibited other purposeful talk behavior.

Clearly link decisions and talk behavior to meaning making.

(chart continues on the next page)

Lesson Plan (cont.)

Stopping place	Cue for getting the talk started	Desired-response possibilities
Precious Habitats	What are you thinking? What is important to think and talk about in this section? Does this build on our thinking after talking about the first section?	My partner and I didn't really understand how the coral grows, so we reread and talked to try to make sense. We think we understand now. But we know the part about fishing with dynamite is bad—the author tells us it's bad, and we agree, because it hurts the coral. Yea, we talked about the dynamite, too. We think it would hurt more than just the coral, and we agree with the author, too. The dynamite and the pollution come from people, and it made us feel bad. We think that's what the author wants. He told about this on purpose because he wants people to stop.
Warming Waters	What are you thinking? What is important to think and talk about in this section? Does this build on our thinking after talking about precious habitats?	My partner and I remembered that the picture at the top shows what happens when the water is warm, so we talked about that. We were trying to figure out what makes the water warm. We think it might be global warming, even though the author doesn't say it. We know that the author is still trying to make us worry about the coral reef because he cares about it.
It's Time to Help	What are you thinking? What is important to think and talk about in this section? Does this build on our thinking after talking about Warming Waters?	My partner and I talked about the heading, because it's like the author is telling us we have to do something. And, he quoted a scientist, and that's what authors do when they want to persuade us. And he said "scientists believe" because he thinks we'll believe the scientists. We know the author is trying to persuade us, but we agree with him anyway. We want to do something—maybe we can get people to care more about polluting.

Process Debrief: *(State the cognitive processes and talk behavior that enabled the construction of meaning.)*

We were able to construct this meaning because of your thinking and talking. Your decisions about where to pause to think more and talk were very smart. You remembered many of the ways of thinking about our nonfiction reading that we've studied (teacher points to classroom charts), and stopped in places that allowed you to talk about this thinking. You used the text features to plan your reading, and the information in them to form a hypothesis before you even started reading. Then you read and talked to confirm or rethink your hypothesis, understand the information, and determine the author's purpose, point of view, and the decisions the author made based on this. You really listened to your partners and developed your ideas. All of this helped you understand what you read, decide if you agreed with the author, and determine if you should act on the information.

This is the way you and your partner should always plan, read, think, and talk your way through a text. Planning and thinking this way will you help you when you read alone, too.

Releasing responsibility: Process debrief and reflection possibilities

Look for opportunity to highlight partners who talked through the information just to understand it and found more evidence to support their theories about the author's purpose, and made any other decisions about what to discuss that enabled strong meaning making.

Look for opportunity to highlight partners who listened with intent, formed ideas, and exhibited other purposeful talk behavior.

Clearly link decisions and talk behavior to meaning making.

Look for opportunity to highlight partners who made connections to information that was not in this text and then discussed it, related the information to information in the visual features, and made any other decisions about what to discuss that enabled strong meaning making.

Look for opportunity to highlight partners who listened with intent, formed ideas, and exhibited other purposeful talk behavior.

Clearly link decisions and talk behavior to meaning making.

Look for opportunity to highlight partners who were talking about the author's choices and ways of persuading, their own beliefs, and any other decisions about what to discuss that enabled strong meaning making.

Look for opportunity to highlight partners who listened with intent, formed ideas, and exhibited other purposeful talk behavior.

Clearly link decisions and talk behavior to meaning making.

Meaning Debrief: *(This is the meaning that students constructed.)*

We think this text is really about the negative effect of human behavior on the environment. This author wants us to know that we can take action and stop the damage to the environment, particularly the coral reefs. We feel like the author is taking a persuasive stance because of specific choices he made, and many of us agree with his point of view (one of many possibilities).

Notes and Reflection: *(State observations that help with the design of future lessons, the text selection, small-group support, and/or individual student support.)*

- The text was engaging and supportive.
- The students' decision making was strong.

Lesson Narrative

As soon as the text appeared on the document camera, it was clear that a wise choice had been made. The students were captivated by the photographs and immediately began studying them, reading captions, and skimming headings. Don launched the students into decisions about how to best approach the text. They read and discussed the title, captions, and photographs, and then constructed an initial understanding very close to what we had anticipated.

We join the thinking and talking as the class finishes reading the first section of text.

Mr. Reed: *What do you and your partner need to think and talk more about? Be sure to honestly listen to each other and keep ideas alive; develop your ideas as much as possible before moving on. When we come back together, I'll ask partners to share what they're thinking and what they talked about to construct that thinking.*

A low roar begins to build as the students turn to each other and begin to talk. Don observes for a moment and then moves decisively to a partnership that seems to be faltering. He asks each partner what he or she is thinking, focuses the students on one idea, and leaves them talking. From there, he checks in on several partnerships, listening in to support and decide which partnership has ideas strong enough to kick off the whole-group conversation.

Mr. Reed: *Let's come back together and discuss our understanding of this section, and how partners thought and talked together. Alex, will you start us off?*

Alex: *What we're saying is that, like, he...he cares... he really wants to take care of the coral reef.*

Mr. Reed: *Shawnee, what did you and Alex talk about that helped you develop this idea?*

Shawnee: *Well, it's because we…um…what?*

Alex: *No, I know! It's because we were talking about that sentence—that one right there (pointing and reading from the text),"But danger looms."*

Shawnee: *Oh, yeah! Because before that, in the first part, he said how everything was all beautiful. He said "beautiful" and "bright."*

Alex: *But then he changed and made it all scary-like. He's worried about it (the coral reefs)! So we think that's why he wrote this.*

Mr. Reed: *So a very smart choice—partners noticing and talking about the author's word choice and how his word choice changed. Did any other partnerships talk about this?*

A chorus of "Yes!" "We did!" and "Oh, yeahs!" reverberate around the circle.

Miranda: *We talked about the same thing, and we think the author wrote it like that on purpose to get us worried, too. It goes with the title—like how he said "crisis."*

Devin: *Yeah, she (Miranda) said that, and I didn't agree— well, not when she said it; but we went back to read it again, and the author tells us the reefs could die in 20 years. Because the photographs are really cool, we don't want it to happen. The author put that photograph there on purpose, huh (looking at partner for confirmation)?*

Miranda: *Yeah, that was smart!*

Mr. Reed: *What did other partnerships talk about?*

Chantel: *We talked about pollution. People pollute sometimes. Well, not on purpose, but it's like everybody drives their cars and stuff. The author says it's giving the danger to it (the reefs). It could make people feel* *bad. He did that probably to make us stop. I think it is persuading, like we said before we read.*

Mr. Reed: *So it sounds as if we're thinking the coral reefs are a beautiful place that's in trouble. You're noticing choices the author made to get you thinking about this. You stopped to think and talk more about those choices and build on your theory. You were careful to listen to each other and develop your ideas. Some of you, like Devin, even changed your mind after listening and talking with your partner. Did you and your partner make smart choices and talk in ways that helped you build strong meaning? (quick process debrief)*

Partners look at each other, most shaking their heads yes, but a few shrug or look sheepish. Don observes and makes a mental note of this. He'll know which partnerships to visit when students begin to talk after the next section. "Hold onto your thinking, and let's read the next section as we had planned."

By the end of the lesson, the students had many opportunities to practice making decisions, thinking, and talking using cognitive processes and talk behaviors that had been heavily supported in the read-alouds. Don ended the lesson with a reminder that they had used many of the strategies on their chart to guide their thinking and talking, and this could be continued while they read and talked with their partners about their own texts. We knew the students would need many more shared opportunities, brimming with feedback, to help them develop independence. Regardless, we planned to begin checking for evidence of these ways of thinking and talking during their partner talk that very day.

Guided Reading

As we work side by side with our students during shared instruction and assess their abilities to take some responsibility for thinking and talking purposefully, we will notice students who are very close to taking control of specific ways of thinking and talking about their reading—but not quite. We know that targeted instruction with slightly less support is what these learners need in order to take on a greater degree of independence. Guided instruction, pinpointing these more precise needs and grouping students with similar needs and reading levels, is the next step on the release of responsibility continuum. In guided reading, our role shifts to coach as we nudge students to use the cognitive processes they are on the verge of controlling.

While shared reading may be whole-group or small-group instruction, guided reading is by definition a small-group format. In guided reading, we design lessons that allow students to read, think, and talk their way through a text together using specific cognitive processes. As with so many of our classrooms, Don's fourth-grade class is composed of students whose reading spans a wide developmental range. To offer lessons designed to meet students' precise needs at their instructional reading levels, they are placed into flexible guided-reading groups determined by reading level and assessed next steps with cognitive processes.

As an added bonus, these groups become an ideal arena for supporting specific students in their next steps with using talk as a constructivist tool. The small size allows for individual coaching with specific talk behavior needs, such as confidence, negotiating entry into the conversation, holding back to give others a chance to express their thoughts, or listening with intent. For many students, it is in this small-group format that they not only refine their abilities with cognitive processes but also find their voices and begin to polish their abilities with purposeful talk.

As the class settles about the room, Don calls five students to gather for guided reading. This particular group, which includes three English language learners at the intermediate level of language acquisition, is hovering at guided reading levels N–O (slightly below-grade level). They are focused on moving beyond understanding isolated facts and bits of information in nonfiction texts toward synthesizing the information into bigger ideas.

Despite the similarities in their comprehension needs, the group presents a range of abilities with purposeful talk. Two of the students, Anthony and Phillip, are strong talkers. They are able to listen with intent and hold onto their own thinking while they engage with the other's ideas. They think quickly and are confident, so their voices are often the first ones heard. Melinda listens with intent and builds on ideas when the teacher is orchestrating and supporting, but tends to revert to saying anything that comes to mind, or "popcorn thinking," without support. A fourth student, Abraham, is quite a smart thinker, but views talk as a contest. He wants to talk first, be right, and be done. Sebastian, an English language learner, is very capable but hesitant to join in the talk and has trouble negotiating entry into the conversation, even in small-group discussion. He seems to be intimidated by the stronger talkers. When he does get excited enough to share his thinking, he will wave his hand in the air, whispering the teacher's name in an appeal to be called on.

Don knows that Sebastian needs to learn to insert his voice and his ideas into the conversation on his own. Abraham needs to learn to listen with intent and value other's ideas. Melinda must begin to self-monitor for listening and keeping lines of thinking alive. Anthony, Phillip, and Abraham might need to hold back to give others (specifically Sebastian) a chance. This affects the way Don prepares the students to read and the way he initiates a conversation after they read.

When the students are preparing to read the first section of the book, Don looks slowly around the circle at each student. "When we're done," he reminds them, "we're going to talk about how this information goes with what we just read and talked about together, and work to build our thinking toward a big idea. Take time to think and have an idea—or even just the beginning of an idea—ready to share. Okay, Sebastian?" This reminds Sebastian of his responsibility to join in the conversation and helps him begin to think in a way that will prepare him to talk.

While the students are reading, Don observes and leans in to coach when necessary. When everyone has read, he turns to Phillip, Abraham, and Anthony, who are jumping up and down with ideas, and says, "Phillip, Abraham, Anthony—why don't you ask Sebastian what he's thinking to start us off?" They protest slightly, but comply, remembering their specific talk focus. Before Sebastian can speak, Don turns to Melinda and Abraham and says, "Melinda, Abraham—are you ready to listen?" After Sebastian shares his idea (and before Abraham is able to dismiss it and share his own), Don turns to Sebastian and says, "Why do you think that, Sebastian? Abraham, let's listen to his reasons and talk more about this."

While all of this may sound overwhelming, it is actually a very fast-paced and natural part of the lesson. The ease with which Don supports each student's talk behavior stems from the fact that he knows the students as learners very well. He's not consulting notes about what each student needs because they talk together often every day. He knows their talk behaviors as well as he knows their reading preferences and favorite topics.

To support the transfer to independence, the lesson debrief is crucial. Just as with read-alouds and shared reading, the guided-reading lesson must be debriefed through the dual lens of the meaning that was constructed and the process of constructing it, including talk behavior. The talk behavior piece must be very explicit, with each student understanding the way in which his or her own talk behavior contributed to the meaning making.

Partner and Independent Reading

As students draw closer to independence with shared and guided instruction, we simultaneously design lessons that teach them to continue reading, thinking, and talking successfully with partners and increasingly on their own. Reading partnerships are an opportunity for students to practice reading, thinking, and talking about text independently—almost. Partnerships are a last step along that release of responsibility slide before we ask students to begin using conversations sparked by specific ways of thinking to generate critical independent thinking.

Together, partners take greater responsibility for decisions about text choice, progression through the text, when to talk, and what to talk about. They learn together to reflect on the degree and quality of their construction of meaning, the strength of their process, and their next steps. A partner gives students continued support, but this is no longer proficient support. This is the support of a co-learner, and success requires an equal amount of input and effort from both—and a great deal of purposeful talk.

Instruction that enables successful partnerships, which is most often in the form of quick mini-lessons, may be procedural, such as learning to select text together, or finding a spot in the classroom to read, think, and talk together. Or, it may be a continuation of the release of responsibility for previous instruction with cognitive process focuses and talk behavior, such as reminding the students to use charting in the room as support. Many teachers find success with a brief "fishbowl" activity during the reading workshop. This is when the teacher has some students in the room pause and gather around a partnership for a quick observation, or look into the fishbowl, and debrief of the pair of learners engaged in successful practice.

When teaching partnerships to our youngest learners, we start them off working side by side, a book shared between them. At first, the partners will lean heavily on each other, reading out loud to each other or reading silently until they are ready to pause and talk. In kindergarten and first grade, when students are reading relatively short texts, this may simply be at the end of the book. As texts become lengthier and more complex, we may structure partner talk to occur at the end of every page or every other page. But again, this is a very artificial structure. Over time, the understanding of when to pause, think more deeply, and talk, which the students are developing in shared and guided instruction, should transfer to partnership work so that students begin taking responsibility for pausing to think and talk based on need rather than a pattern.

Older students who are new to partnerships may likewise begin by working side by side with their partners. However, more proficient readers will most likely not want to read out loud together—nor should they. Proficient readers need the flexibility to scan ahead, reread, and speed up or slow down as dictated by the complexity of the text and their own construction of understanding. What seems to work best, if possible, is having duplicate copies of texts available. This way, partners are able to sit together to talk when the text demands a conversation, but each has his or her own copy for comfort and control.

Gradually over time, we ask students to take responsibility for more reading and thinking independently. As Dorn and Scoffos explain, "The true test of learning takes place when a student applies the knowledge, skills, and strategies gained from teacher-assisted lessons to independent work" (2001, 9).

During independent reading, we encourage students to construct meaning using the cognitive processes they have been practicing and the echoes of past conversations in order to read critically. Of course, we still want students to value and seek purposeful talk with others about their reading and thinking. Even during independent reading, the students balance their reading with partner talk.

We interact with the students during partner and independent reading by conferring while they are reading and talking, and during workshop shares. Our role shifts into a mix of teaching, coaching, nudging, and offering feedback, depending on the needs of the student. While there are no precise lesson plans for these opportunities to further support our readers, the teacher enters into every interaction with a wealth of information to work from, including a clear understanding of the instructional journey the class as a whole has progressed through and the individual strengths and needs of each student. We begin by initiating a conversation that would give us insight into the processes (cognitive and purposeful talk) the students are using, those they are neglecting, and the resulting level of understanding being constructed. As always, we offer specific feedback that supports partners and individuals in reflecting on and refining their practices.

Just a week after the shared-reading lesson using *Coral Reef Crisis*, our fourth graders were transitioning from shared reading to partner and independent reading. Students hurried about the room, gathering their texts, book logs, and sticky notes. Duo by duo, they settled in for a partner talk before heading off to read independently.

In this particular fourth-grade classroom, the students have taken on a pattern of meeting with their partners for an initial conversation, heading off for somewhat more independent reading, and then joining back together to discuss important aspects of their thinking and to strengthen the construction of meaning. I say "somewhat more independent reading" because each student is thinking about the text with the support of a progression of conversations with his or her partner, and they have the flexibility to lean over and talk with their partners at any time should excitement or confusion necessitate it.

This flow from partnership support to independent effort and back was very purposeful. We wanted the students to continue to build competence and value thinking and talking together to construct the strongest understanding possible, yet also learn how to have those "in the head" conversations that enable readers to construct strong understanding even when reading alone.

The initial conversation ensures that students start to read with some predictions, expectations, a purpose and a plan, and most importantly, some sharing of ideas in general, which begins the co-construction process. Partners meet anywhere from a few quick minutes to perhaps as long as 10 minutes, depending on what it is they need to think and talk about.

While reading independently, the students are thinking toward a conversation at the end of the workshop. This means they may be quickly jotting down ideas, questions, or ah-ha moments on sticky notes or in reading logs in anticipation. Knowing that they will meet again with their partners for conversation after reading independently helps encourage the active, engaged reading required to build a habit of mind for those times when they read alone.

The students were in their initial partnership meeting and, as usual, Don and I stood back to observe for a moment before diving into conferring. Seeing no immediate concerns, we headed toward Trevian and Alejandra, who were continuing with a text they had started the day before, a stunning narrative nonfiction text titled *Animal Scavengers: Army Ants* by Sandra Markle (2005). As we sat down next to them, the two were talking about the amazing photos.

Trevian: *This one's pretty cool.*

Alejandra: *Kinda sick and cool. Ahhh! Remember this one (holding up a close-up shot of an ant's head)?*

Mr. Reed: *What are you two thinking and talking about?*

Trevian: *Well, the author had all these really cool— yeah, sick, cool photos, and all the facts told about jobs the ants do. We think the author is informing, because there's lots of facts.*

Alejandra: *Yeah, but the facts are like amazing things we don't know. So maybe the author is telling them so we think how good ants can work. She thinks the ants aren't all gross, like we think. We go, "Oh no, ants!" (this line acted out with an 'eeeek!' expression).*

Trevian: *Yeah, like when they're in our classroom.*

Alejandra: *But she thinks these ants are really smart. That's her point of view.*

Ms. Nichols: *How did you decide what to think more and talk about to figure this out?*

Alejandra: *Mostly it's the facts. Some of them we didn't get because there's some really hard words. So I put stickies when I didn't know, so we could talk. And every time we talked, we couldn't believe ants could do that.*

Trevian: *Yeah, all the facts make us go, "I can't believe it!"*

Ms. Nichols: *So the author's choice of information—what* *facts are included—helped you understand her purpose and point of view. What sounds really important is that you used your talk time to make sense of challenging vocabulary and facts and then wondered why the author included the information. What do you think about ants now?*

Trevian: *I don't know. They're kinda cool, I guess.*

Ms. Nichols: *Have you thought and talked about the way the author's ideas are affecting you?*

Trevian: *(Looks at Alejandra and shakes head no.)*

Ms. Nichols: *Remember, as readers, we always want to think about the way a text affects us—decide what we think and will do with the information. Do you think that's your next step?*

Trevian: *So we can read again today and think about that—okay? (looking at Alejandra)*

During this conference, I gave Alejandra and Trevian feedback on a specific decision that had worked well for them and pointed out next steps to strengthen their understanding of the text and the use of the information in it.

At this point, most of the students were transitioning into independent reading, so Don and I took a moment to survey the room again, observing carefully. Who settled into their reading immediately, and who was having difficulty engaging? Who was jotting down notes, preparing for the partner conversation to come? Who leaned over to talk with his or her partner? What was the effect of each of these behaviors on the construction of meaning? In part, this observing was to help us note individuals who need an immediate conference to get started, or the need for future procedural mini-lessons. However, we also knew that illustrations of strong learning behavior were fodder for workshop shares and were always on the watch for possibilities.

Next we joined Melinda and Anthony, two readers who often

needed extra support and were still engaged in partner talk. They were reading *One Whole Day: Wolves*, a lyrical text by noted naturalist Jim Arnosky (2001), who invites the reader along to observe the day-long activities of a pack of wolves.

Anthony: See, I wrote a sticky note here because the author writes it (the text) like the panther book.

Melinda: I wrote on mine that…

Mr. Reed: Hold on, Melinda, did you really listen to what Anthony said?

Melinda: He said that he wrote that…about the panther book? What did you say?

Anthony: That he (the author) wrote the way that the panther book was.

Melinda: Oh, yeah! It's…it's…it's that way like a poem (eyes searching the poster). What do you call it?

Mr. Reed: Why do you think Jim Arnosky wrote the text in a lyrical way?

Anthony: (shrugs)

Melinda: It's because he wants us to be calm, like with the panther. So we don't think they're scary.

Mr. Reed: So, Melinda, you really listened to Anthony's idea, and the two of you stayed focused on it and talked more about it. Now you both understand something about this text and what the author is doing that you didn't understand before. Melinda, you had a sticky note to talk about, too. Anthony, be ready to really listen to Melinda's idea.

Don stayed with this partnership for a few more minutes, coaching their talk behavior, then offering another layer of feedback on their efforts to listen with intent and keep a line of thinking alive. He prepared them for independent reading, making sure they both understood exactly what they were going to be thinking about and preparing to talk more about as they read.

Clearly, this partnership required more supportive coaching than that of Trevian and Alejandra. This range of abilities within partnerships will exist in every classroom. Some partners simply need suggestions, while others can actually take on new challenges beyond the work of the rest of the class. Other partnerships need support ranging from coaching to teaching in order to enable them to continue their journeys toward independence.

Next, Don's attention was drawn to Phillip, who was sitting on his own, flipping slowly through the pages of *The Life Cycle of an Earthworm* by Bobbie Kalman (2004). He was obviously not reading, yet deep in thought. As Don sat down next to him, Phillip anticipated his question and started talking.

Phillip:	*Look! I looked at the headings, here…see…the table of contents shows them. The last one says "helping," like in the books when the author is persuading and wants to get us to help. I decided to read that first to see if he's persuading.*
Mr. Reed:	*What did you decide?*
Phillip:	*Well, yeah, he is persuading because he tells you that you can help. He tries to get us to do it.*
Mr. Reed:	*Persuading you to think or do what?*
Phillip:	*Um…care maybe? Or help? Probably help, because people step on worms and stuff.*
Mr. Reed:	*So how does flipping through the pages help you figure this out?*
Phillip:	*Sometimes authors use the photos to help with persuading. See, like on our chart. So I'm*

	checking the photos to see if they're persuading, too.
Mr. Reed:	*So, Phillip, I'm hearing that you discovered that this author used some persuasive tools. But you don't seem to know what the author is persuading you to do or think. Your next step seems to be to figure that out. How will you go about that?*
Phillip:	*I guess read?*
Mr. Reed:	(Shaking head yes) *Then you can talk with Sebastian* (his partner) *about the author's purpose in very specific ways—be able to say exactly what you think the author is persuading you to do or think, how you know, and whether or not you are persuaded.*
Phillip:	*Should I tell Sebastian?*
Mr. Reed:	*Would it be a stronger conversation if you both read and thought about it before you met?*
Phillip:	*Yeah! I'll tell him now…*

Don recognized that Phillip was attempting to independently use what he had learned about determining an author's purpose to better understand the specific choices the author had made. He routed Phillip into his next steps, preparing him for successful independent reading and a strong partner conversation after the reading.

To state the obvious, students need to take responsibility for an enormous range of planning, decisions, and ways of thinking and talking. The key to success is a gradual release of precise increments of the work over time, along with informative feedback that enables students to reflect on their efforts and continually strengthen them, thus making smarter choices.

© Shell Education

Chapter 4

Maintaining the Momentum with Purposeful Talk

It is close to winter break (or it could be close to spring break, or Groundhog Day, or…), and months of careful planning designed to teach the use of purposeful talk are behind you. You're feeling good about the students' progress—or at least, you had been. Then a read-aloud falls apart. Everyone is talking, no one is listening—or no one is talking or listening. Partner talk becomes either an unruly uproar or uncharacteristically silent.

Talking with others for the purpose of constructing meaning is complex work, both academically and socially. Even with the strongest instruction aimed to explicitly enable purposeful talk, predictable problems with talk behavior will arise. Sometimes we see the trouble coming—a steady march of little situations with warning flags popping up along the way. Other times, the trouble creeps up on us—and the students seemingly lose their abilities with purposeful talk overnight.

One possible cause may be inconsistency on our part. We're tired or distracted—and not as vigilant in our orchestration of the talk. We allow ideas to float away in the air without digging into them. We tolerate a student who talks over another or permit ideas not closely connected to the construction of meaning to hijack the conversation. Or the many and varied demands of the classroom result in planning that is just not as tight as it needs to be to ensure continued success with purposeful talk.

Sometimes the difficulties with purposeful talk can be attributed to changes in the classroom community. The little conflicts that arise when we spend so much time together in close quarters may begin to chip away at the emotional environment, or we find that new students entering the classroom have changed the class dynamic.

Conversely, the strength of our work with purposeful talk may actually create new dynamics—both social and academic—that we had not anticipated. With so many possible origins for difficulties with purposeful talk behavior, we must step back to observe and assess problems when they occur, and then take positive steps to put the talk back on track. What follows are a few of the most predictable problems or vexing patterns of behavior with purposeful talk—those that seem to arise in a variety of classrooms across grade levels. While there is no single solution that will work for every group of students in every classroom, the suggestions included are the products of successful interventions thoughtfully crafted by teachers in varied contexts.

A Focus on Purposeful Talk Slips Away

As students' abilities with purposeful talk grow, it is quite easy to begin taking their competence for granted, forgetting that newly formed behaviors are not yet habits; they require consistent nudging and nurturing to truly take hold. Additionally, with a variety of student needs to consider as we design each lesson, then monitor and adjust during the course of the lesson, it's quite possible that our focus on purposeful talk could unintentionally lose its intensity. That said, when we notice students slipping back into their old habits of participation prior to focusing on purposeful talk, our investigation into causes often must start with our own efforts with lesson design, consistency in focusing fully on what the students are saying during the lesson, and precision in orchestrating the talk.

Are we taking time to consider what we hope the students will be thinking and talking about, and designing lessons in ways that necessitate this thinking and talking? Are we not only orchestrating the conversation, but noting the level of support students need with the orchestration? Are we designing lessons that continually release responsibility for aspects of the thinking and talking to the students? Taking time to reflect on our role in students' continued progress with purposeful talk might enable us to solve the difficulties we're seeing simply by refocusing ourselves.

Slipping Back into the "Right Answer" Paradigm

Nothing stifles the sharing and development of ideas faster than a sense that the question being pondered has one acceptable right answer. While there are obviously questions that do have a single correct answer, our process for constructing meaning of compelling texts should be most often guided by a true exploration of possibilities. This enables students to use their talk behavior for real purposes and prepares them for a way of approaching their learning and the world that will promote open-mindedness and deeper understandings.

For many of us, however, this way of constructing knowledge is a shift from our own school experiences. And while we work diligently to create lessons that allow for diverse understandings to be explored, old habits die hard. When struggles with talk are evident, we may need to check our own responses to ideas to be sure we haven't locked in one correct interpretation, thus discouraging the exploration of other possibilities.

Community Difficulties

The creation of a supportive learning community is a pivotal factor for students' academic success. The creation of our learning communities does not come easily at the start of the school year, and once created, strong communities require constant nurturing and upkeep. If our community weakens, and students no longer feel safe in the classroom environment or no longer believe that their ideas will be treated with respect, they will not continue to risk sharing their thinking. When students seem to have lost the trust and respect necessary for purposeful talk to thrive, we need to first search out the root of the problem.

Any reassessment of our classroom community needs to begin with a quick check of ourselves. A smart first step is ensuring that we are modeling the same degree of respect for others and their ideas that we are hoping to see our students exhibit. Once we are reassured that our own behavior is supportive of our students' efforts, we shift the focus to the students' behavior, watching for any sign of interactions that stifle the sharing of ideas. When we do spot a problem behavior, we begin the process by helping the students see the behavior and understand how it affects their efforts to think and talk together. Adding another reflective layer to the lesson design to discuss the cognitive process focus and purposeful talk behavior, as well as the students' reactions to others and their ideas, helps create this awareness.

If there is not enough time for this during and after the lessons themselves, separate classroom meetings are an attractive option. During these meetings, we bring specific lessons back to life by reminding students of the focus, as well as the mix of the talk and behaviors that helped the class to construct strong understanding and those that impeded that construction. During these meetings, it is important for students to begin to tease apart the behaviors and develop their own understandings of those that are supporting their goals and those that interfere. In this way, they refine their own understanding of a strong learning community and the behaviors that allow both the community and their learning to flourish.

Partnership Woes

Partnerships are an integral support structure for developing independent ability. The formation of strong partnerships requires close observation of students' learning behaviors and thoughtful decision making. To create these partnerships, we pair students of similar reading ability, similar preferences in text selection, and compatible personalities. Our goal is to form partnerships that endure over time so that students build a history of shared texts, conversations, and ideas to draw on as they read, think, and talk together.

That said, there is also a benefit to learning to read, think, and talk over time with an assortment of individuals. For this reason, we do switch partnerships at key points during the year, such as shifts in our units of study, returning from long holiday breaks, or at points at which students' maturity levels and likes and dislikes seem to be changing.

There are times during the year, however, when partnerships should be building strength, but instead, a pair or two are having difficulty. Sometimes the reasons for the difficulties are academic. One student may have made leaps in his or her reading level, resulting in partners who are no longer comfortable with the same level of text. Or, one student may be having difficulty with one or a progression of the cognitive focuses and is struggling to understand while his partner becomes frustrated.

Or, the problems may be social in nature. One or both students may be having difficulty with the behavior necessary for their efforts to be fully focused on the academic work and the talk behavior necessary to keep the thinking and construction of meaning moving forward. This results in either the weakening of both partners' behaviors or one partner again frustrated because the other is not holding up his or her end of the thinking and talking.

If a partnership is struggling because of differences in academic ability, we need to decide whether this is the most productive learning situation for the two students. While it's advantageous to have a stronger colleague lift the level of another's thinking and talking, this needs to be a give-and-take relationship with each partner at times lifting the other. We don't want a partnership situation where one student is essentially constructing meaning on his or her own, and the other becomes either frustrated or passive because the efforts are being shouldered by the more proficient peer.

When a partnership begins showing signs of difficulty for social reasons, we assess the situation, offer support, and involve the students in the process of regaining control. Supporting the partners in giving each other reminder cues, developing goals together, and teaching them to reflect on their own learning behavior together may be enough. If not, a partnership change may be the best option. While we do not want to give up on a partnership too easily, knowing that a change means disrupting another partnership, we also don't want the students to spend more time on trying to work through problems than on thinking and talking together.

Talk Dominators

As adults, we know the talk dominators among us. They're the people we tend to avoid conversationally because we never get a word in edgewise. Talking with these friends or colleagues is more of a verbal mugging than a stimulating give and take of ideas.

In classrooms where students are given the freedom to speak without raising their hands, certain students will emerge whose thinking comes quickly, who are quite sure of themselves, and who are clearly capable of negotiating entry into the conversation. At times, this strength crosses the line, and these capable thinkers and talkers end up controlling the majority of the talk time. Quite simply, they dominate the classroom conversations.

Often we exacerbate this problem because many of these talk dominators have strong ideas, and we rely on their thinking to up the level of the construction of meaning. If they aren't talking already and the effort toward understanding is falling flat, our talk dominators are our go-to kids.

When talk dominators begin to overshadow other class members and stifle the flow of ideas, awareness is our best ally. We begin with developing the understanding that we all function differently as learners. Some students (and adults, for that matter) need to process their thinking out loud right away, while others like to mull things over silently for a moment. In addition to needing a few seconds to mull things over, some class members may be translating their thinking into English or searching for the right words to express a sense of something they just can't articulate yet. Based on the content and context, individuals may have an immediate reaction to an idea, or they may need to rethink what they just heard to make sense of it before they're able to express anything that pushes the construction of meaning.

Then, to help students develop an awareness of their own

patterns of participation, we pause during the course of our conversations to notice whose voice is being heard, and how often. Quite often, our talk dominators are stunned at how frequently they are talking in relation to others in the class. Talk comes so naturally to them that they simply are not aware.

As our talk dominators develop awareness, we begin coaching their talk habits. We remind them to hesitate before speaking to see if someone else has an idea, allowing shy students or those not as strong at negotiating a turn to talk first. We cue them to actually invite others into the conversation and notice when the body language of a peer indicates that they are trying to negotiate a turn to speak.

We will never completely squelch our talk dominators, nor do we want to. We simply want to develop awareness and refine their "purposeful talk manners" so that the flow of ideas becomes more balanced.

Shy Students

Of course, nothing aggravates the plight of our shy students more than the talk dominators. Our shy students often have brilliant ideas; what they lack is the confidence to voice them.

Far and away, the biggest support we can create for our shyest students is a strong emotional environment. Knowing that their classroom is a place where risk taking is valued and their ideas will be supported by their peers (and by the teacher) is a start. A supportive partner can also serve as a bridge to the larger conversation. Many shy students will talk to a single trusted colleague far more readily than to the whole class.

Once shy students are talking to partners, sharing their thinking in small-group instruction may prove a challenging but doable next step. Our guided-reading or small-group shared reading lessons become venues in which we support them in gaining the confidence to speak. As they develop confidence with a group, they will also experience the power of adding to conversations in positive ways, feeling their own thinking grow stronger as a result.

During this process, offering shy students the gentle encouragement of their peers without being made to feel as if they are "center stage" is crucial. This means inviting them into the conversation when they are truly excited by an idea and encouraging them to share their thoughts. What we don't want to do is put the student on the spot, insisting that he or she speak when there are no ideas burning inside, while the others wait restlessly.

We may not be able to change our shy students into the confident learners we hope they will become in just one year's time, but we can support them in experiencing the power of sharing their thinking and the joy of using their talk to construct meaning with others.

Who's in Charge?

Regardless of the strength of the developing purposeful talk abilities, we often find that our students direct their ideas to us rather than to each other. Even when responding to another's thought, they will focus their gazes directly at the teacher as they speak. This may be due to a mix of factors, including years of patterns of learning that involved answering teacher questions, a strong sense of the teacher as the ultimate authority in the classroom, or students' desire for teacher support as they voice their thinking.

Another possible cause is that we've taken too heavy a hand in orchestrating the talk and crossed the line into oversupporting, and ultimately controlling, the talk. This happens when we respond to every thought from the students ourselves, repeating, rephrasing, strengthening, or pushing back. If we are to release responsibility for purposeful talk to the students, we must lessen our control, orchestrating the talk when necessary and then backing out of the talk when we are not needed.

So when the talk seems to flow from student to teacher rather than from student to student, we start the problem solving both by looking at our pattern of participation and by having the students consider the dynamics of a natural, spontaneous group conversation.

We might pose a common scenario to the students. "You're at lunch, talking with a group of friends about a movie. Whom do you look at while you talk?" The students naturally respond, "Everybody!" "How would it feel if you looked at just one person while you talked?" we query. Then we try it. We pull a small group together and get them talking about something, with the instruction that they can only look at one person in the group as they talk. Of course, this seems very odd and rapidly becomes very silly. But what's important is that the students realize right away that this isn't comfortable. It is not how we behave while we are talking. We discuss the social reasons for looking around the group, such as the desire to include everyone. We also discuss the reasons based on meaning-making, such as the need to gauge reactions from all involved.

Then we work to make the current talk dynamic in the classroom visible. As we think and talk our way through a text, we pause to ask students whom they were looking at as they spoke. They catch on pretty quickly. And from this realization, we begin to practice the art of eye contact. We speak directly to someone if we are responding to them and use our eyes to include all in the conversation by sweeping our gaze slowly around the circle. This can feel very contrived at first, but it is a valuable habit the students must develop if they are to learn to use talk purposefully in other structured arenas.

And as the students work to be responsive to one another, we work to monitor our own role in the talk. Often, we do need to question, clarify, and bundle ideas in ways that help students hold onto them. However, at other times, we can remain silent and look around the circle in anticipation, thus teaching students to respond directly to one another.

Length of Conversations

The stronger that students become with their purposeful talk, the more they begin to value processing their thinking with others, therby creating longer lessons, debriefs, and general conversations.

Often during lessons, the students will have used purposeful talk to reach the understanding the lesson was designed for but still have a need to talk further. And all too often, we are faced with a decision between allowing students the leeway to talk to suit their needs and the need to move on to meet the demands of the academic day. The teacher in us doesn't want to turn off the flow of ideas, but the classroom manager in us constantly has an eye on the clock. With the impossibility of all we need to fit into the day, the realization that we need progressively longer periods of time for conversations can cause us to shake in our boots.

One possibility for dealing with this situation is teaching students to pause in a conversation, hold onto the constructed meaning up to that point, and continue the discussion during other times—independent or free-choice times, when walking to and from the library—the possibilities are actually quite numerous. Nothing is more stunning than picking the students up from lunch and having them fill you in on the continuation of a conversation they enjoyed while they were eating! Remember, the goal of all this work is to enable just this degree of independence. When a topic is so compelling that continued talk is not only possible but bubbling forth, why not plant the seed and see what happens?

What seems to be consistent when righting wobbles with purposeful talk is the need to continually assess and revisit purposeful talk behavior and involve the students in reflections on their own evolving abilities and the end result of thinking and talking together. This not only strengthens the students' abilities to use talk as a constructivist tool but may also actually prevent further wobbles.

Chapter 5

What Can Be

It was late June and another school year was winding to an end—Katie Crommer's second year of teaching her students to talk purposefully. As I tiptoed in for a last visit, the students were embedded in a conversation initiated by a read-aloud of *Dad, Jackie, and Me* by Myron Uhlberg (2005). The group had paused midway into the author's note at the end of this realistic fiction that explained that the story was based on the author's memories of his father, who grew up in a deaf residential school in the early 1900s, and the great Jackie Robinson. The students' talk was teetering between understandings about the story and using this understanding, although still incomplete, to better understand their world and their ability to shape it.

Monique: *So that's how the story…it isn't really true… not all of it…but the reasons he wrote it—those are true.*

Keshawn: *But there really was the Dodgers. They're true.*

Shaun: *But it isn't about the Dodgers. The author is saying about racism.*

Monique: *And not just if you're black—that kind of racism. He's talking about everybody—like how they treated his dad. He couldn't learn baseball because he was deaf.*

Juan Carlos: *He's saying to us to behave better to people even if they're different.*

Monique: *It's what we talked about at recess. How if kids…if we don't let them play, then we're like those people.*

Joshua: *So yeah, we hafta let everybody play—like if we play soccer. We don't want to be like how they are. (This was based on a separate conversation earlier in the week about including students from the special education class in their games during recess.)*

This was a huge understanding for the students to live and grow by, and what made it all the more powerful is that they had constructed it themselves. As the conversation drew to a close, Katie asked the students to use their reading logs to reflect on their talk behavior.

I waited a few moments as the students settled, then headed toward Monique, who had jotted down a few words and was staring up at the ceiling. Knowing Monique well and her pattern of participation (talk dominator extraordinaire), I slid into the chair next to her to peek at her reflection up to this point and to chat. She had written, "My talk behavior today was…" and now the rest of what she needed seemed to be on the ceiling.

Ms. Nichols: *What are you thinking?*

Monique: *Well, I'm trying to get what to write. My talk was kinda good today. I tried not to be a dominator, and I asked Shaun and Dareanna what they were thinking because we hadn't heard their voices yet. Everybody respected all the ideas. Well, a few people didn't listen, but we talked about that, and Shaun—he had really good thinking, and it made us all talk a lot, and all of it made me change my mind.*

Ms. Nichols: *Wow, so why don't you know what to write?*

Monique: *It's because we kinda had a problem because some kids still didn't talk. So we didn't hear all the good ideas, maybe.*

Ms. Nichols: *Why didn't they share their thinking?*

Monique: *I think it's maybe because we still don't be sure to ask the shy people. We get busy talking and forget. They may think we don't care how they think.*

What's notable here is that Monique's thoughtful reflection reveals the value she places on thinking and talking with her peers. Echoed throughout are traces of class conversations intended to tackle difficulties with talk, an awareness of herself as a dominator, awareness of shy students or those who need support in entering the conversation, and the realization that we don't always listen to and respect ideas. This awareness may soon become the catalyst that will encourage Monique to begin orchestrating conversations more purposefully herself.

Monique and her classmates did not begin the year with this degree of reflective ability and this much respect for the power of purposeful talk. It was developed through lesson design with dual cognitive process and purposeful talk focuses, lessons that brought the thinking and talking along the release of responsibility slide toward independence, and an abundance of feedback.

Our hope for Monique and her classmates is that they will find the same degree of focus and effort around purposeful talk in their classrooms in the years to come. Imagine the thinking and talking, the ability to construct deep understandings of texts and the world, and the degree of independence these students will have if they continue to learn together in environments that value the use of talk as a constructivist tool.

Planning Form for Teaching Purposeful Talk Behavior to Support the Construction of Meaning—Lesson Plan Template

Cognitive Process Focus: *(This is the way(s) of thinking and talking about reading that the students are learning in order to support the construction of meaning.)*

Text:

Introduction: *(Include the cognitive process focus, the talk behavior that will be used to develop ideas, and text introduction.)*

Stopping place	Cue for getting the talk started	Desired-response possibilities

Process Debrief: *(State the cognitive processes and talk behavior that enabled the construction of meaning.)*

Purposeful Talk Focus: *(This is the talk behavior the students are focused on in support of the construction of meaning.)*

Goal: *(This is the meaning that students are thinking and talking toward.)*

Introduction *(cont.):*

Anticipating talk difficulties	Supports if the construction of meaning is not progressing

Meaning Debrief: *(This is the meaning that students constructed.)*

Notes and Reflection: *(State observations that help with the design of future lessons, text selection, small-group support, and/or individual student support.)*

Appendix B

Planning Form for the Release of Responsibility for Thinking and Talking About Texts—Lesson Plan Template

Cognitive Process Focus: *(This is the way(s) of thinking and talking about reading that the students are learning in order to support the construction of meaning.)*

Text:

Supports: *(What aspects of this text will help students make meaning?)*

Introduction: *(What will I say to set up the reading through the lens of our focus and meaning making?)*

Stopping place	Cue for getting the talk started	Desired-response possibilities

Process Debrief: *(State the cognitive processes and talk behavior that enabled the construction of meaning.)*

Purposeful Talk Focus: *(This is the talk behavior that the students are focused on in support of the construction of meaning.)*

Goal: *(This is the meaning that students are thinking and talking toward.)*

Challenges: *(What aspects of this text might interfere with meaning making?)*

Introduction *(cont.)*:

Releasing responsibility: Process debrief and reflection possibilities

Meaning Debrief: *(This is the meaning that students constructed.)*

Notes and Reflection: *(State observations that help with the design of future lessons, the text selection, small-group support, and/or individual student support.)*

References Cited

Allington, R., and P. Johnston. 2001. *Reading to learn: Lessons from exemplary fourth-grade classrooms*. New York: The Guilford Press.

Arnosky, J. 2001. *One whole day: Wolves*. Washington, D.C.: National Geographic Society.

Bohm, D. 1996. *On dialogue*. New York: Routledge.

Brown, S. 2004. *Shared reading for grades 3 and beyond: Working it out together*. Wellington, New Zealand: Learning Media.

Bruer, J. T. 1994. Classroom problems, school culture, and cognitive research. *In Classroom lessons: Integrating cognitive theory and classroom practice*, ed. K. McGilly. Cambridge, MA: MIT Press.

Burleigh, R. 2007. *Stealing home: Jackie Robinson: Against the odds*. New York: Simon & Schuster.

Calkins, L. M. 2001. *The art of teaching reading*. New York: Addison-Wesley.

Cazden, C. B. 2001. *Classroom discourse: The language of teaching and learning*. Portsmouth, NH: Heinemann.

Center on English Learning and Achievement. 2006. Raising the level of student engagement in higher order talk and writing. http://cela.albany.edu/research/partnerb3.htm.

Clarke, S. 2003. *Enriching feedback in the primary classroom*. London: Hodder & Stoughton Educational.

Dorn, L., and C. Scoffos. 2001. *Shaping literate minds: Developing self-regulated learners*. Portland, ME: Stenhouse.

Fox, M. 2000. *Harriet, you'll drive me wild!* New York: Harcourt, Inc.

Kalman, B. 2004. *The life cycle of an earthworm*. New York: Crabtree Publishing.

London, J. 2000. *Panther: Shadow of the swamp*. Cambridge, MA: Candlewick Press.

Markle, S. 2005. *Animal scavengers: Army ants*. Minneapolis, MN: Lerner Publications Company.

References Cited *(cont.)*

Nichols, M. 2006. *Comprehension through conversation: The power of purposeful talk in the reading workshop.* Portsmouth, NH: Heinemann.

Otaiba, S. A., and J. Torgeson. 2007. Effects from intensive standardized kindergarten and first-grade interventions for the prevention of reading difficulties. In *Handbook of response to intervention: The science and practice of assessment and intervention,* ed. S. R. Jimerson, M. K. Burns, and A. M. VanDerHayden, 212–22. New York: Springer.

Pearson, D., and M. Gallagher. 1983. The instruction of reading comprehension. *Contemporary Educational Psychology* 8 (March): 317–44.

Peterson, R. 1992. *Life in a crowded place: Making a learning community.* Portsmouth, NH: Heinemann.

Resnick, L. 1999. Making America smarter. *Education Week Century Series* 18 (40): 38–40. http://www.edweek.org/ew/vol-18/40resnick. h18.

Simich-Dudgeon, C. 1998. Classrooms strategies for encouraging collaborative instruction. http://www.ncela.gwu.edu/pubs/directions /12.htm

Uhlberg, M. 2005. *Dad, Jackie, and me.* Atlanta, GA: Peachtree Publishers.

Vygotsky, L. S. 1978. *Mind in society: The development of higher psychological processes.* Harvard, MA: Harvard University Press.

Wolf, M. K., A. C. Crosson, and L. B. Resnick. 2004. How classroom talk supports reading comprehension. *Reading Psychology* 26 (1): 27–53.

Woodson, J. 2001. *The other side.* New York: Putnam Books.

Woolley, M. 2003. *Playing outside.* South Yarra, Australia: Eleanor Curtain Publishing. Okapi Educational Materials, http://www.myokapi.com.

Write Time For Kids. 2000. Huntington Beach, CA: Teacher Created Materials.

© Shell Education